Practical Guides for Beer Quality

FLAVOR

D0746515

Charles W. Bamforth
University of California, Davis

AMERICAN SOCIETY OF
Brewing Chemists

Front cover photograph is © Artem Myazin/Shutterstock.com

Library of Congress Control Number: 2013948962
ISBN: 978-1-881696-23-0

© 2014 by the American Society of Brewing Chemists
Second printing 2014

Printed in the United States of America on acid-free paper

American Society of Brewing Chemists
3340 Pilot Knob Road
St. Paul, Minnesota 55121, U.S.A.

For Lucie Jane Firman

This Book and This Series

This is the second volume in a six-part series addressing quality issues of beer. There are, of course, a number of books and many articles that address such matters. This particular series might be viewed as a set of user manuals, much like the handbook that accompanies your car.

In each book I seek to address individual quality issues from a standpoint of

- the basic underpinning science (without getting too complex and grinding the grist too fine),
- the practicalities of the issue pertaining to brewing and its associated activities,
- quality assurance and quality control parameters, and
- a troubleshooting guide.

Contents

The Flavor of Beer: Nobody Said It Was Easy

As a quality assurance manager it was in my job description to handle customer complaints. Maybe it was letters with varying degrees of emotion received from those buying our bottles or cans and finding something amiss. Sometimes it was a landlord or pub manager who had a grievance. Either way, the gripes very rarely concerned the flavor of the beer. In small pack (i.e., cans or bottles) it might be a foreign body (including the famous occasion—truly a precautionary tale—when we were accused of packaging a can with a condom). Or perhaps it was a greater or (usually, to be fair to us) lesser degree of turbidity. Most frequently—especially in the case of pubs—it was mutterings about the foam, and we saw in the first book of this series how that problem usually lay at their door, not ours.

Now let's make one thing clear: there were relatively few complaints in total, a tiny fraction representing much less than 0.1% of all the beer we produced. Of that small number, I recall only a single instance of a flavor complaint. The reality is that most consumers don't feel qualified to mutter deprecating comments about a beer tasting "wrong" because, frankly, they are not perfectly sure of the ground on which they stand. Is the beer *supposed* to taste that way? Do they simply believe that an occasional flavor change away from what they *think* they are used to is inevitable and, therefore, tolerate it on those grounds? Any idiot can see whether there are bubbles or not on a beer, but is one running the risk of ridicule by questioning the taste and smell of a product?

In fact, an appreciation of beer flavor is very much a personal issue. I would never want judgmental assertions of which beer is good and which is bad to be declared by self-appointed experts with the pompous pretentiousness that suffuses the description of wine. You have only to read the self-righteous and intolerant declarations of a Robert Parker or an Alice Feiring (and their opinions are poles apart in themselves) to appreciate just how far dogmatic belief in what is right and what is wrong can go.

I contend that for beer (just as for wine) the preferred flavor of a product is entirely a matter of personal preference. It is perfectly acceptable to like subtly nuanced North American light lagers: that does not make you a bad person. Equally, if you favor a product that might reasonably be described as hefeweissen meets blackest stout with a hefty dose of IPA thrown in for good measure, perhaps further complicated by a dollop of *Brettanomyces*, then that is okay, too. Each to his or her own.

To the question "what is a good beer?" I am wont to reply, "the one that you enjoy." Nobody has the God-given right to declare what is a beer nirvana and what is gutter swill. Rather, we should rejoice that there is a huge diversity of beers to enjoy, covering all manner of aromatic and flavorful possibilities.

The real requirement, to my mind, is to determine for yourself as a brewer what you seek to deliver in your product and then to strive to deliver that flavor profile every time. In other words, the goal is **consistency**.

I am fond of recalling the e-mail I received from someone who, wearied of my insisting on such regularity from batch to batch, declared that he liked surprises. I asked in return whether he would like the vicarious excitement of not knowing whether his car would pull off the forecourt after filling it with gas. Was it a good batch of fuel or not? In fact, the only product that springs to mind as inevitably a surprise package is wine. Hence the ridiculous rituals of the affected pour and, even more irritating, the opportunity for wine writers to spew forth their overstated tosh.

Surely it makes just as much sense to insist upon batch-to-batch regularity in flavor as it does to demand that every brew must deliver the same quality of foam, the same color, and the same clarity?

Mention of these quality attributes draws attention to how what the customer sees—and hears—impact the perception of beer flavor. Years back, when a notable English brewer changed away from fermenting in Burton Union systems to more easily cleaned fermenters, the famous ale was deemed as tasting different by those whose belief systems could not countenance change and who were in denial of all the work that the company did to demonstrate a perfect flavor match.

It goes beyond that. When an iconic North American lager brand was bought by a major competitor a few years ago, the aficionados proclaimed that the lager wasn't as good, even though all the evidence indicated that the transition did not materially affect the beer. Indeed, it was now probably being brewed with a far greater quality assurance presence.

It's all in the mind—just as it was years ago for me when I saw a mouse scurry across a pelmet in an Indian restaurant in Cheshire. It's amazing how the palatability of the lamb pasanda deteriorated for me at that precise point.

Imagine, if you will, that you are in the supermarket. There are just two tins of tomato soup left on the shelf. One is pristine, whereas the other has a slight dent in it or a small tear on the label. You will inevitably choose the undamaged one, even though you know full well that the liquid inside is going to be as expected in both cans. And so it is with beer. Given a choice between a scuffed returnable glass bottle and a pristine virgin one, the perception will be that the beer is better in the latter.

We have already seen in the first volume of this series how people will declare that the flavor of a beer with a better head is superior. I contend, too, that an unexpectedly turbid beer will raise questions in the mind of the consumer about flavor. (And although we haven't done the research, I rather suspect the converse to be true: that a customer who ordered a hefeweissen and found it lacked turbidity would instantly make judgments about the authenticity of its flavor.)

The extent to which most people are subconsciously influenced by the appearance of beer or wine is highlighted by the approach of Hoby Wedler, a blind chemist and gifted taster, who runs Tasting in the Dark events (Sidebar 1-1).

Back in the 1980s we did simple trials coloring up a lager with a tasteless dye (Table 1-1). Blind tasting showed no differences, but when tasters looked at the trial and control beers, they judged their flavor differently, declaring the darker product to have ale characteristics.

Tasting in the Dark

I speak in this chapter of the impact that the appearance of the package and the product can have on the perception of flavor. In fact, I am often wont to say "we drink with our eyes."

What if, though, we cannot see? In that case, we are obliged to make our judgments of beer quality on the basis of what our palates and noses tell us.

Enter Hoby Wedler, an astonishing young man who has been blind from birth (www.ls.ucdavis.edu/mps/news-and-research/hoby-wedler.html). Apart from being a gifted scientist who is (as I write) pursuing a Ph.D. in organic chemistry, he also is a talented taster. Hoby has developed for the Francis Ford Coppola Winery in Geyserville, California, a remarkable interactive presentation called Tasting in the Dark (www.examiner.com/article/experience-wine-tasting-the-dark). His audience is blindfolded as he guides them through the tasting of a range of wines, highlighting the diversity of tastes and aromas that can be perceived. Ahead of this event, Hoby has used his acute sensory skills to identify the various flavors that he can detect, and he uses this information to produce reference samples that are presented to the blindfolded tasters to emphasize the range of characters that they should be expecting to find.

I had the privilege of being a part of the first such session that Hoby ran in the brewing industry for an audience of over 100 salespersons for a national company. Earlier in the day, following recipes Hoby provided, a group of us put together the reference standards in small jars—for example, some orange zest, mango, cilantro, and cumin might be popped into the jars in appropriate amounts and then "muddled." These were later passed among the blindfolded tasters, and Hoby led the discussion of what could be perceived. Then it was on to the beers, looking (as it were) for those same characters in the products and delving into the likely identity of the beers. Hoby proceeded then to articulate the likeliest food pairings with those beers—he is quite the chef.

Tasting in the Dark is a truly powerful experience, one that really emphasizes how the absence of visual clues forces you to pay particular attention to the senses of smell and taste.

TABLE 1-1.

The Influence of Color on Flavor Perception[a]

Taster	Standard Lager (Sample A)	Standard Lager Plus 9 Units of Color (Sample B)	Difference	Comments on Sample B
1	2.0	5.1	+3.1	Quite astringent, more burnt, more bitter. Lacks DMS of sample A.
2	6.1	6.5	+0.4	More bitter.
3	3.0	7.3	+4.3	
4	4.5	8.1	+3.6	Malty, no DMS.
5	6.7	6.7	0	
6	1.6	5.9	+4.3	Less sharp, duller flavor.
7	1.3	1.8	+0.5	
8	3.2	8.3	+5.1	Bitter, diacetyl, full, heavy.
9	2.0	2.7	+0.7	
10	6.2	4.6	−1.6	

[a] Scores out of 10. 1 = most lager-like. 10 = most ale-like. Adapted from Bamforth et al (1989).

The simple reality is that we have to specify carefully all of these quality parameters for a beer (package, foam, clarity, and color) if we are to control perceived flavor.

Accepting these multiple impacts on the perception of flavor, in this volume I will focus specifically on the aroma and taste of beer. Here, I am considering beer at the point in time that the brewer would prefer the beer to be consumed. For most beers, that is as soon as possible after the beer has been filled into its container. The flavor of most beers deteriorates from that point on, but that will be the subject matter for the third volume of this series.

Trusting Our Senses

Accepting that what our eyes suggest to us heavily sways our perception, what are the *direct* ways in which we detect the flavor of a beer? We can divide perception into three categories: pain, taste, and smell.

Next to water and alcohol, the most abundant chemical constituent of beer is carbon dioxide (CO_2), which we detect as pain. It represents pleasing, almost masochistic suffering. This gas, just like chili peppers, mouthwash, menthol, and onion vapor, acts as a *chemesthetic*. Such materials interact with our nerve fibers (the trigeminal sense) either directly or indirectly (Fig. 2-1). In the case of CO_2 we register this interaction as tingling—and we like it. The more CO_2, the more the tingle.

Most of a beer's flavor is detected by taste buds on the tongue and especially through the aroma registered via olfactory receptors in the nose. In case you doubt the role of the nose in all this, I suggest you grab a clothespin and clip your nostrils together before sipping a pint of beer. You will soon discover that the flavor delivery is severely restricted.

This is why I urge you to pour beer into a glass (and not only for the sheer hedonistic ecstasy of seeing the foam, as described in the first volume of this series). As you tip the beer in the act of drinking, your nose is exposed to the vapors emerging from the drink. By sipping from a bottle or can directly, you do not get this aromatic experience. Maybe

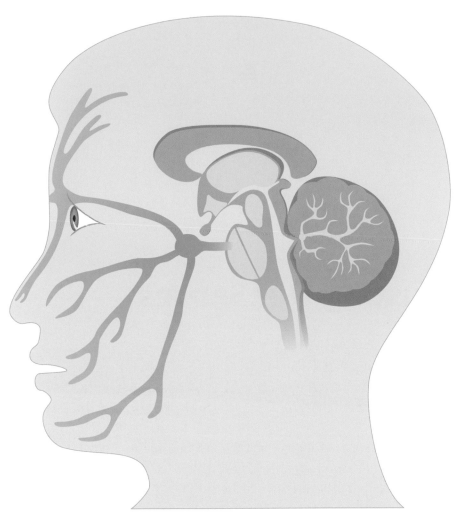

Fig. 2-1. The various branches of the trigeminal nerve. It is the nerve responsible for sensations in the face and determines functions such as biting and chewing. In the context of detecting the pain response owing to carbonation, we are mostly concerned with the branch leading to the palate. Adapted from image © Alila Medical Media/Shutterstock.com.

such an approach is okay for a bland beer, but it is certainly not recommended for any ale or lager from which you desire an all-encompassing flavor perspective.

Once in the mouth and certainly during the act of swallowing, the vapors also drift up the passage at the back of the throat that leads directly into the nasal regions (Fig. 2-2). So, if you like, there are three stages at which you appreciate the volatile components of beer: in an initial sniffing, as the beer is being transferred from the tilted glass into

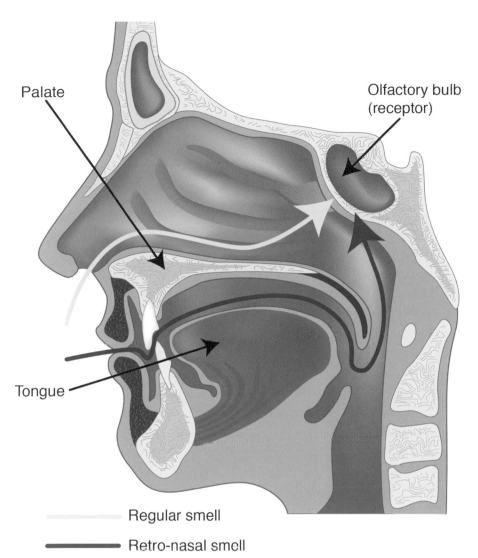

Palate

Olfactory bulb
(receptor)

Tongue

Regular smell

Retro-nasal smell

Fig. 2-2. Two different routes for perceiving smell. Adapted from image
© Yoko Design/Shutterstock.com.

your mouth, and then as the beer is moved around in the mouth and swallowed.

Received wisdom has it that there are only four key tastes as detected by the mouth: sweet, salt, sour, and bitter. The Japanese throw in a fifth, *umami*, which is most simply described as "moreish," as exemplified by monosodium glutamate in Chinese food. Most experts on the human ability to detect taste accept umami as a fifth taste sensation.

It has been handed down that there are specific taste buds on the tongue for the four (or five) major flavors. Moreover, it has been emphasized over the years that there are specific concentrations of such taste buds in different regions of the tongue, with those detecting sweetness being particularly located at the tip, those for saltiness at the tip and around the sides of the tongue, sour at the sides but not the tip, and bitterness buds right at the back.

We now know that this representation is oversimplistic and that within a single taste bud there are receptor cells that sense sweet but also others that register saltiness, sourness, bitterness, and umami.

We don't need to get hung up on this complexity, short of saying one more thing: the buds probably detect more than these classic tastes. For example, I am firmly convinced that I can detect the cardboard nature of aged beer more readily by taste than by smell. It works in reverse, too. One of the neatest ways to detect iron in a beer is not by looking for a metallic taste. Instead, make one of your hands into a fist and rub a bit of beer onto the flesh between the base of the thumb and the forefinger. Then smell the skin. You can smell the metallic quality more readily than taste it. I have no idea why.

In short then, there is a tremendous complexity involved in the flavor appreciation of beer. Perhaps we should not stress too much about it but rather leave the scientists studying the senses to delve ever deeper, while we simply get on with the task of using whatever tools our body has (nose, tongue, and nerves) to interpret as a continuum the flavor impact of our ales and lagers.

The Flavors of Beer

Without sweating too much, then, about quite how we detect them, what are the flavors of beer?

Naturally, as the exciting craft sector in the United States gratifyingly burgeons, this question becomes more and more difficult to answer. It seems that not a day goes by without an entirely novel brew being presented to the populace, flavored with yet another innovative ingredient. Traditionally—and, sometimes, not so traditionally—a rich diversity of flavor-impacting materials may feature in beer, from chili to chocolate, pumpkins to pomegranates. Gruit (an herb mixture sometimes spelled grut) has been rediscovered.

For the most part, an addition of this nature will deliberately be made with the intention of it being readily identifiable in the beer. Black cherries in kriek and lemon in shandy, for example, unmistakably deliver their inherent aroma characteristics. Recognizing that there are endless possibilities that we cannot hope to cover completely, let us restrict our discussion to the flavor delivered by what we might describe as the mainstream components of a brew, namely, cereal, water, hops, and microorganisms.

The most famous representation of the aroma and taste of beer is the flavor wheel (Fig. 3-1). It was the brainchild of joint working groups from the American Society of Brewing Chemists, the Master Brewers Association of the Americas, and the European Brewery Convention

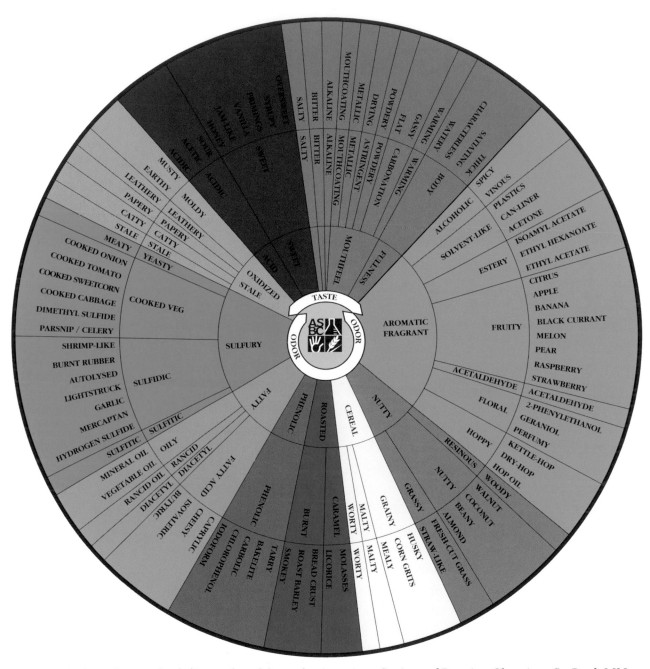

Fig. 3-1. The beer flavor wheel. (Reproduced from the American Society of Brewing Chemists, St. Paul, MN. An individual Beer Flavor Wheel may be purchased at asbcnet.org/flavorwheel.)

12

and reported in a short paper by Morten Meilgaard, Charles Dalgliesh, and John Clapperton (1979). The aims were, first, to enable brewers to communicate effectively about flavor and, second, to name and define each separately identifiable flavor note in beer. They reckoned that 44 terms met the first objective and suggested an additional 78 terms for the second purpose. In a comprehensive table reproduced here (Table 3-1), they listed each term with some initial recommended reference standards (extended in a 1982 paper by Meilgaard and two other co-workers). Interestingly, and not often remarked upon, they indicated that most of the components contribute to both aroma and taste (compare that statement with the points made in chapter 2).

The wheel has stood the test of time, although there was a suggestion to improve upon the mouthfeel component of the diagram (see chapter 5). As such, it is a tried and trusted tool for brewers to use to describe the aroma and taste of beers. Perhaps, however, it is not as sexy as the equivalent wine wheel, which is rather better fitted for the purpose in using more pleasing terminology to convey flavor information to customers and laypersons.

In chapter 4 we will explore the types of sensory work that can be employed to arrive at a meaningful description of the flavor of any given beer and the techniques that can be applied to ensure that the desired aroma and taste are delivered time and again for that beer.

TABLE 3-1.

Recommended Descriptors[a]

Class Term	First Tier	Second Tier	Relevance[b]	Comments, Synonyms, Definitions	Reference Standard
Class 1 — Aromatic, Fragrant, Fruity, Floral					
	0110 Alcoholic		OTW	General effect of ethanol and higher alcohols	Ethanol, 50 g/L
		0111 Spicy	OTW	Allspice, nutmeg, peppery, eugenol; see also 1003 Vanilla	Eugenol, 120 µg/L
		0112 Vinous	OTW	Bouquet, fusely, wine-like	(White wine)
	0120 Solvent-like		OT	Like chemical solvents	
		0121 Plastics	OT	Plasticizers	
		0122 Can-liner	OT	Lacquer-like	
		0123 Acetone	OT		(Acetone)
	0130 Estery		OT	Like aliphatic esters	
		0131 Isoamyl acetate	OT	Banana, peardrop	(Isoamyl acetate)
		0132 Ethyl hexanoate	OT	Apple-like with note of aniseed; see also 0142 Apple	(Ethyl hexanoate)
		0133 Ethyl acetate	OT	Light fruity, solvent-like; see also 0120 Solvent-like	(Ethyl acetate)
	0140 Fruity		OT	Of specific fruits or mixtures of fruits	
		0141 Citrus	OT	Citral, grapefruit, lemony, orange rind	
		0142 Apple	OT		
		0143 Banana	OT		
		0144 Black currant	OT	Black currant fruit; for black currant leaves use 0810 Catty	
		0145 Melony	OT		(6-Nonenal, cis- or trans-)
		0146 Pear	OT		
		0147 Raspberry	OT		

[a] From Meilgaard et al (1979), with minor differences in formatting.
[b] Particular relevance: O = odor, T = taste, M = mouthfeel, W = warming, and Af = afterflavor.
[c] Quercitrin is both astringent and bitter.

continued

TABLE 3-1. continued

Recommended Descriptors[a]

Class Term	First Tier	Second Tier	Relevance[b]	Comments, Synonyms, Definitions	Reference Standard
		0148 Strawberry	OT		
	0150 Acetaldehyde		OT	Green apples, raw apple skin, bruised apples	(Acetaldehyde)
	0160 Floral		OT	Like flowers, fragrant	
		0161 2-Phenylethanol	OT	Rose-like	(2-Phenylethanol)
		0162 Geraniol	OT	Rose-like, different from 0161; taster should compare pure chemicals	(Geraniol)
		0163 Perfumy	OT	Scented	(Exaltolide musk)
	0170 Hoppy		OT	Fresh hop aroma; use with other terms to describe stale hop aroma; does not include hop bitterness (see 1200 Bitter)	
		0171 Kettle-hop	OT	Flavor imparted by aroma hops boiled in kettle	
		0172 Dry-hop	OT	Flavor imparted by dry hops added in tank or cask	
		0173 Hop oil	OT	Flavor imparted by addition of distilled hop oil	

Class 2 — Resinous, Nutty, Green, Grassy

Class Term	First Tier	Second Tier	Relevance[b]	Comments, Synonyms, Definitions	Reference Standard
	0210 Resinous		OT	Fresh sawdust, resin, cedarwood, pinewood, sprucy, terpenoid	
		0211 Woody	OT	Seasoned wood (uncut)	
	0220 Nutty		OT	As in Brazil nut, hazelnut, sherry-like	
		0221 Walnut	OT	Fresh (not rancid) walnut	
		0222 Coconut	OT		
		0223 Beany	OT	Bean soup	(2,4,7-Decatrienal)
		0224 Almond	OT	Marzipan	(Benzaldehyde)
	0230 Grassy		OT		

continued

TABLE 3-1. continued

Recommended Descriptors[a]

Class Term	First Tier	Second Tier	Relevance[b]	Comments, Synonyms, Definitions	Reference Standard
		0231 Freshly cut grass	OT	Green, crushed green leaves, leafy, alfalfa	(*cis*-3-Hexenol)
		0232 Straw-like	OT	Hay-like	
Class 3 — Cereal					
	0310 Grainy		OT	Raw grain flavor	
		0311 Husky	OT	Husk-like, chaff, *Glattwasser*	
		0312 Corn grits	OT	Maize grits, adjuncty	
		0313 Mealy	OT	Like flour	
	0320 Malty		OT		
	0330 Worty		OT	Fresh wort aroma; use with other terms to describe infected wort (e.g., 0731 Parsnip/celery)	
Class 4 — Caramelized, Roasted					
	0410 Caramel		OT	Burnt sugar, toffee-like	
		0411 Molasses	OT	Black treacle, treacly	
		0412 Licorice	OT		
	0420 Burnt		OTM	Scorched aroma, dry mouthfeel, sharp, acrid taste	
		0421 Bread crust	OTM	Charred toast	
		0422 Roast barley	OTM	Chocolate malt	
		0423 Smoky	OT		
Class 5 — Phenolic					
0500 Phenolic			OT		
		0501 Tarry	OT	Pitch, faulty pitching of containers	
		0502 Bakelite	OT		
		0503 Carbolic	OT	Phenol, C_6H_5OH	

continued

TABLE 3-1. continued

Recommended Descriptors[a]

Class Term	First Tier	Second Tier	Relevance[b]	Comments, Synonyms, Definitions	Reference Standard
		0504 Chlorophenol	OT	Trichlorophenol (TCP), hospital-like	
		0505 Iodoform	OT	Iodophors, hospital-like, pharmaceutical	
Class 6 — Soapy, Fatty, Diacetyl, Oily, Rancid					
	0610 Fatty acid		OT		
		0611 Caprylic	OT	Soapy, fatty, goaty, tallowy	(Octanoic acid)
		0612 Cheesy	OT	Dry, stale cheese, old hops; hydrolytic rancidity	
		0613 Isovaleric	OT	Dry, stale cheese, old hops; hydrolytic rancidity	(Isovaleric acid)
		0614 Butyric	OT	Rancid butter; hydrolytic rancidity	Butyric acid, 3 mg/L
	0620 Diacetyl		OT	Butterscotch, buttermilk	Diacetyl, 0.2–0.4 mg/L
	0630 Rancid		OT	Oxidative rancidity	
		0631 Rancid oil	OTM	Oxidative rancidity	
	0640 Oily		OTM		
		0641 Vegetable oil	OTM	As in refined vegetable oil	
		0642 Mineral oil	OTM	Gasoline (petrol), kerosene (paraffin), machine oil	
Class 7 — Sulfury					
0700 Sulfury			OT		
	0710 Sulfitic		OT	Sulfur dioxide, striking match, choking, sulfurous-SO_2	(KMS)
	0720 Sulfidic		OT	Rotten egg, sulfury-reduced, sulfurous-RSH	
		0721 H_2S	OT	Rotten egg	(H_2S)

continued

TABLE 3-1. continued

Recommended Descriptors[a]

Class Term	First Tier	Second Tier	Relevance[b]	Comments, Synonyms, Definitions	Reference Standard
		0722 Mercaptan	OT	Lower mercaptans, drains, stench	(Ethyl mercaptan)
		0723 Garlic	OT		
		0724 Lightstruck	OT	Skunky, sunstruck	
		0725 Autolysed	OT	Rotting yeast; see also 0740 Yeasty	
		0726 Burnt rubber	OT	Higher mercaptans	
		0727 Shrimp-like	OT	Water in which shrimp have been cooked	
	0730 Cooked vegetable		OT	Mainly dialkyl sulfides, sulfurous-RSR	
		0731 Parsnip/Celery	OT	Effect of wort infection	
		0732 DMS	OT	(Dimethyl sulfide)	DMS, 100 µg/L
		0733 Cooked cabbage	OT	Overcooked green vegetables	
		0734 Cooked sweet corn	OT	Cooked maize, canned sweet corn	
		0735 Cooked tomato	OT	Tomato juice (processed), tomato ketchup	
		0736 Cooked onion	OT		
	0740 Yeasty		OT	Fresh yeast, flavor of heated thiamine; see also 0725 Autolysed	
		0741 Meaty	OT	Brothy, cooked meat, meat extract, peptone, yeast broth	

Class 8 — Oxidized, Stale, Musty

Class Term	First Tier	Second Tier	Relevance[b]	Comments, Synonyms, Definitions	Reference Standard
0800 Stale			OTM	Old beer, overaged, overpasteurized	(Heat with air)
	0810 Catty		OT	Black currant leaves, ribes, tomato plants, oxidized beer	(p-Menthane-8-thiol-3-one)
	0820 Papery		OT	Initial stage of staling, bready (stale bread crumb), cardboard, old beer, oxidized	(5-Methylfurfural, 25 mg/L)

continued

TABLE 3-1. continued

Recommended Descriptors[a]

Class Term	First Tier	Second Tier	Relevance[b]	Comments, Synonyms, Definitions	Reference Standard
		0830 Leathery	OTM	Later stage of staling, often used in conjunction with 0211 Woody	
	0840 Moldy		OT	Cellar-like, leaf mold, woodsy	
		0841 Earthy	OT	Actinomycetes, damp soil, freshly dug soil, diatomaceous earth	(Geosmin)
		0842 Musty	OT	Fusty	
Class 9 — Sour, Acidic					
0900 Acidic			OT	Pungent aroma, sharpness of taste, mineral acid	
	0910 Acetic		OT	Vinegar	(Acetic acid)
	0920 Sour		OT	Lactic, sour milk; use with 0141 Citrus for citrus-sour	
Class 10 — Sweet					
1000 Sweet			OT		Sucrose, 7.5 g/L
		1001 Honey	OT	Can occur as effect of beer staling (e.g., odor of stale beer in glass), oxidized (stale) honey	
		1002 Jam-like	OT	May be qualified by subclasses of 0140 Fruity	
		1003 Vanilla	OT	Custard powder, vanillin	(Vanillin)
		1004 Primings	OT		
		1005 Syrupy	OTM	Clear (golden) syrup	
		1006 Oversweet	OT	Sickly, sweet, cloying	
Class 11 — Salty					
1100 Salty			T		Sodium chloride. 1.8 g/L
Class 12 — Bitter					
1200 Bitter			TAf		(Isohumulone)

continued

TABLE 3-1. continued

Recommended Descriptors[a]

Class Term	First Tier	Second Tier	Relevance[b]	Comments, Synonyms, Definitions	Reference Standard
Class 13 — Mouthfeel					
	1310 Alkaline		TMAf	Flavor imparted by accidental admixture of alkaline detergent	(Sodium bicarbonate)
	1320 Mouthcoating		MAf	Creamy, *onctueux* (Fr.)	
	1330 Metallic		OTMAf	Iron, rusty water, coins, tinny, inky	(Ferrous ammonium sulfate)
	1340 Astringent		MAf	Mouth puckering, puckery, tannin-like, tart	Quercitrin, 240 mg/L[c]
		1341 Drying	MAf	Unsweet	
	1350 Powdery		OTM	O—Dusty cushion, irritating, (with 0310 Grainy) mill-room smell TM—Chalky, particulate, scratchy, silicate-like, siliceous	
		1360 Carbonation	M	CO_2 content	
		1361 Flat	M	Undercarbonated	60% of normal CO_2 content for the product
		1362 Gassy	M	Overcarbonated	140% of normal CO_2 content for the product
		1370 Warming	WMAf	See 0110 Alcoholic and 0111 Spicy	
Class 14 — Fullness					
	1410 Body		OTM	Fullness of flavor and mouthfeel	
		1411 Watery	TM	Thin, seemingly diluted	
		1412 Characterless	OTM	Bland, empty, flavorless	
		1413 Satiating	OTM	Extra full, filling	
		1414 Thick	TM	Viscous, *epais* (Fr.)	

Sniffing and Sipping

Powerful tools like the flavor wheel allow experts to articulate what flavors and aromas they perceive in a given beer. However, we must also address what realistically is achievable and desirable in the quantification and descriptiveness of beer flavor on a day-to-day basis, when and where is it important.

I frequently tell the story of an early visit of mine to the tasting inner sanctum of an extremely large brewing company, where I was asked to comment on their flagship brand as brewed in different locations globally. To my palate, the samples (perhaps there were 15) were indistinguishable. Now, around that table were men and women who tasted this brand day in and day out and had done so, in most instances, over lengthy careers. From sheer familiarity and repetition they could detect the subtlest of differences between batches. Thus, they represented a sublime resource in the company's avowed goal to achieve absolute consistency from brew to brew.

The reality, of course, is that the vast majority of beer drinkers do not approach this degree of authority when it comes to tasting any beer. Rather akin to the challenge to distinguish between Coke and Pepsi, I contend that most consumers would be unable readily to tell apart two beer brands of similar style, especially without any visible clues. Sure, I would hope and expect that a taster could differentiate a low-calorie lager from a black IPA. But I question how successful most people would be if presented with three samples each of the three biggest selling light beers in the United States, with the nine beers randomized and presented as a batch of nine and the task being to identify each of those beers. And I am sure the same challenges would present themselves if the beer categories were pilsners or porters or marzens.

I was astonished years ago to be assured by two eminent Guinness people that, when tasted "blind," most consumers are unable to differentiate Guinness Stout from Bass Ale. If these scientists were right, then it speaks still further to my point that (with the obvious exception of a few true experts) most drinkers are not especially skilled at articulating the nuances of flavor. In passing I might (with whatever degree of provocative intent) opine that the same applies to wine.

This truth, it needs to be said, does not excuse the brewer on whatever scale from seeking consistency from brew to brew. As I have stressed repeatedly, few and far between are the consumer products on this planet in which overt batch-to-batch differences are tolerated, or even celebrated. The one product that stands alone is wine.

The question to be addressed is this: do the wine folks actually have a valid stance, one that might be adopted in the world of brewing? The fundamental credo for many in the world of wine is that the grape varies depending on its growth location and the season. Thus, a certain terroir will afford nuances to a wine that should always be recognizable in it, but these will vary somewhat from year to year.

Might that tolerance and even celebration also be reasonable for beer and indeed something to be shouted from the rooftops? Does it go hand in hand with the rustic charms that have brought to us entities like the Slow Food Movement? In an era when too many in the brewing industry use unforgivable words like "industrial beers" to label the output of brewing megacompanies, might a recognition of the agricultural vagaries that can impact on the sensorial characteristics of a product actually be an avenue that brewers, too, should take?

But let us not get too philosophical. Whichever approach a brewer takes—on the one hand the insistence on rigid and absolute batch-to-batch consistency or on the other an acceptance of some degree of variability within the boundaries of what clearly is the flavor of a given brand—we need tasting tools to inform us.

Setting Up for Sensory Testing

Ideally, you will need the following:

- a big enough space that avoids crowding
- a comfortable space (air conditioned, free from distracting aromas, clean, and presenting minimal distractions)
- an adjacent preparation space
- uniform but not intense lighting
- booths for individual tasting (preferred)
- no cell phones, perfume, talking, or eating—minimal distractions
- dedicated glassware that is clean, uniform in size, and clear (unless color is to be disguised)
- samples at a uniform temperature that are dispensed to a uniform size with a uniform head
- randomized presentation of coded samples, with a different code for each taster
- unsalted crackers (or bread) and water for palate cleansing
- avoidance of an excessive number of samples
- no conducting of tasting soon after consumption of food

Basically, we can divide tests into two types: those that require trained tasters and those that do not. The latter are useful if we simply want to know whether two beers differ in their flavor, with no expectation of ascertaining from the tasters what the basis of that difference is. The former have more value, however, as they have much greater utility in helping us craft new brews, interpret the nature of any observed variations, investigate the offerings of other brewers, and much more.

In either case, setting up the tasting area properly is critical. Sidebar 4-1 highlights the key points, and we will discuss them more later in this chapter.

Anybody who plans to participate in descriptive work on beer flavor needs to undertake some form of training. Fundamentally, tasters need to be able to appreciate the four basic tastes—sweet, salt, sour, and bitter—and to recognize the more significant and commonly encountered aroma notes that may be present to a greater or lesser extent, which I venture to suggest are

- banana
- green apple
- hoppy
- grainy
- grassy
- malty
- worty
- burnt
- phenolic (medicinal)
- phenolic (clove)
- butterscotch/popcorn
- rotten egg
- struck match
- canned corn
- catty
- cardboard/wet paper

The most accessible and reliable way to do this sensory training is via kits (see Appendix 1), which usually feature the relevant and responsible chemicals immobilized in cyclodextrins, cage-like molecules that trap the necessary flavors inside. When the powder is mixed with water or beer, the cage opens up, and the aroma is released.

Clearly, people can buy these kits and train themselves. Depending on the size of the company and the number of folks to be trained, it may be worthwhile bringing in a trainer (Appendix 2). Such training is especially useful when aiming for reliable scoring of individual attributes, such as appear in Table 5-3, on significant flavors in hop varieties.

Whether the approach is formal or informal, we need to have confidence that we can recognize the individual key flavor attributes and be able to signify 1) whether each is at roughly the level we expect, 2) whether one or more flavor notes are present at a level somewhat lower than expected, or 3) whether one or more flavors are present at a level above that expected.

It really is a problem if we are "blind" to any given attribute. Being acutely sensitive to a given aroma is less of a concern but one that nonetheless can bring some challenges. Take diacetyl, for example, the molecule that affords the butterscotch/popcorn character to beers. If the person responsible for releasing beer to trade (who in a one-person operation would be **you**) is unable to detect diacetyl at the levels typically registered by others, then beers may be headed into the customer's glass with this (generally considered to be) "off" character. For my part, I am acutely sensitive to diacetyl, to the extent that perhaps I am overly critical about what is or is not acceptable for release to trade. For this reason, it is best that decisions on acceptability are never the preserve

of one person if at all possible. If two or three individuals at least debate the relative merits and demerits of a beer (preferably briefly), then consensus can be arrived at.[1]

Some of the sensory techniques in which these skills come into play can really be rather simple but enormously valuable nonetheless.

When I was the quality assurance manager at a brewery, the most important tasting was the 9 a.m. session every workday attended by me, my lab manager, the head brewer, and his assistant brewmaster. The chap who coordinated the taste work would have the samples ready for us, and we would taste them sequentially. We would each have a half-pint glass and stand (literally) around a bucket. Alan would pour into each of our glasses a couple of ounces of each sample, and we would swirl, sniff, taste, and toss away the excess. Then we would, one by one, announce our scoring for that sample on a four-point scale:

1 – zero defects; on target; beer can go ahead

2 – marginally off target (and we would say in what way); beer can go ahead

3 – significantly off target (and why); beer to be held, further analyzed, and a decision made regarding what to do when more information is at hand

4 – major defects (and why), beer unacceptable, so dispose of it; urgently put in place systems to make sure it won't happen again

I can remember only once that we had a 4—a case of serious iron pick-up off a filter.

---

[1] Of course, there is the reality in some companies of the executive palate. In my old company one of my bosses was a cigar aficionado. This penchant tended to dull the acuity of his senses when it came to beer but certainly did not dull his authority on what was or was not acceptable flavorwise. Another senior executive (who, unlike the first, was an unpleasant man) was accused of heading up a brewery that produced a low-alcohol beer with a pronounced diacetyl nose. The beer measured high for diacetyl by gas chromatography. The company headquarters expert taste panel declared the lager to be registering high for butterscotch. Nonetheless, he arrived at headquarters, sniffed and tasted the offending product, and—rather like Nelson putting the telescope to his blind eye—declared, "This beer does not smell of butterscotch." The senior corporate management would not overrule him, and the beer went into the market. I don't recall a single complaint from a customer.

We tasted beer at the end of fermentation (and the company philosophy was that vicinal diketone control was a fermenter event), postfiltration but prepackaging, and postpackaging. In this way we ensured that unacceptable beer did not proceed to the next stage, incurring on-cost, if it was going to be identified as unacceptable down the pike. For example, how stupid would it have been for us to package that metallic-tainted beer?

Building on that point, our daily samples also included water: the water as it arrived at the brewery and that which had had something done to it, for example, deaeration for the dilution of high-gravity brews. The rationale is obvious: the vast majority of beers are largely water. If that water has a taint, it would be stupid to use it. (The same applies, of course, to other raw materials, and some brewers are more fastidious than we were in doing taste tests on other brewing materials, process ingredients, and even packaging materials. More on measuring flavor in chapter 6.)

Table 4-1 summarizes some of the difference tests that have been proposed, and Table 4-2 describes some descriptive tests. Arguably, there is a direct correlation between the size of the company and the numbers of methods that will be applied and the extent to which they will be used. For instance, difference testing is going to be much more widely employed in companies with more than a single brewery—for example, to ascertain whether there is a statistically significant difference between the same brand of beer produced at two different locations.

I think it is important for us to be quite clear about how much effort it is sensible to put into **formal** tasting work, even at the largest of brewing companies. I have absolutely no doubt about **informal** tasting: it is critical. The round-the-bucket procedure I described earlier is a personal favorite, and I would argue that it is the right approach even for a tiny brewery with one guy or gal at the bucket.

At the other extreme, as a scientist I am always enormously irritated when I read sophisticated scientific papers reporting sensory studies that do not give full details of how the work was done: how many tasters, their degree of training, the number of replicates, and the statistical techniques employed. Absent this information, it is impossible to know whether any differences being reported have any meaning. I will stress this point in the next volume when we talk about studies on flavor stability.

TABLE 4-1.

Difference Tasting Techniques[a]

Test	Description
Three glass (triangle)	Tasters are given three beers, two of which are identical, and they are asked to select the odd one out. Tasters may be asked to provide some descriptive comments (ASBC Sensory-7).
Duo-trio	Tasters are presented first with a reference beer and then with two other glasses of beer, and they are asked which of these two matches the reference (ASBC Sensory-8).
"A" or "not A"	Tasters are presented with a reference beer ("A") and then with several glasses that may or may not be A. They are asked to say whether each sample is or is not A.
Two out of five	Tasters receive five glasses of beer, two of one batch and three of another. They are asked to sort them.
Paired comparison	Tasters are presented with two glasses containing different batches of the same beer and are asked to nominate which beer is more intense in a given flavor note, or are asked without prompting to say what the difference is (ASBC Sensory-6).
Difference from control	Tasters are given a sample of control beer and another beer and are asked to score the magnitude of the difference between them on a scale of 0 (no difference) to 9 (extremely different) (ASBC Sensory-13).

[a] For an elegant description of sensory evaluation techniques above and beyond what is included in this chapter, including issues of statistical significance, see Simpson (2006).

TABLE 4-2.

Descriptive Tasting Techniques[a]

Test	Description
Flavor profile	Trained tasters score beers for a range of flavors (compare with the flavor wheel), scoring each attribute on a scale (perhaps 1–5) or by marking on a horizontal line from "absent" to "intense" (ASBC Sensory-10).
Trueness to type	Tasters score beers for individual attributes in comparison with the target for that beer according to a scale of 0 (on target), −1 (slightly less than expected), −2 (much less than expected), +1 (slightly more than expected), and +2 (much more than expected).
Ranking test	To put a series of samples into sequence in terms of an individual flavor descriptor (ASBC Sensory-11).

[a] For an elegant description of sensory evaluation techniques above and beyond what is included in this chapter, including issues of statistical significance, see Simpson (2006).

But day-to-day life in a brewery is not about detailed and statistically robust research. Sensory work in a brewery is surely about ensuring that we are striving toward zero defects and production of all batches of beer with a satisfactory flavor profile (i.e., at or close to expectation). Although statistics can come into it, what we are much more concerned with is the confidence that the tasting work we are doing on raw materials and products will, when allied to process control and specifications, assure quality output.

The ideal is a trained, reliable, articulate group of regular tasters (with enough numbers to allow absences for reasons of vacation, sickness, and so on) who meet at the appropriate times and locations to perform sensory work one step beyond the bucket and provide expert commentary on all the products from the brewery.

No matter whether tasting is a solitary occupation or involves troops, it is important that proper attention is paid to what I call time, terrain, and technique.

Time: it is not a good idea to do tasting after meals, especially those featuring strongly flavored foods, or even after coffee breaks.[2] Morning is best.

Terrain: tasting should be in a place with minimal distractions and no interfering smells (see ASBC methods Sensory-1 through Sensory-5). If the aim is to make a judgment specifically on matters of flavor, then it is best for the tasting to be such that no visible clues are offered by the beer (foam, color, and clarity), so the tasting could be in a room lit by red light and the beer dispensed into dark glasses. There should not be sample overload for fear of fatiguing the senses. The use of tasting booths in which tasters are separated is desirable for tasting protocols that do not involve interaction and dialogue (Fig. 4-1).

Technique: test samples in ascending order of flavor intensity. With a glass no more than a third full, swirl. Take a few short sniffs and then one or two longer inhalations. Take a sip or two and swirl. Finally, swallow and breathe out through your nose.

At each of these individual stages, be looking variously for whatever elements of mouthfeel, taste, and aroma you register.

---

[2] Or any other type of break, such as one that took place when I was running a session somewhere in Oregon. That was a "weed" break. I stayed indoors.

Fig. 4-1. Individual tasting booth. Photo courtesy of Aroxa.

The Molecules of Flavor and How They Find Their Way into Beer

The story is told of how legendary Nobel Prize–winning biochemist Sir Hans Krebs was once addressing a group of young students on the topic of how he had unraveled the tricarboxylic acid cycle (also known as the Krebs cycle), which is at the heart of respiratory metabolism. Drawing attention to the starting point as pyruvic acid, he turned to write the formula on the board, hesitated, pivoted around, picked up his notes, and *copied* the structure onto the blackboard.

If Krebs couldn't remember the formula for pyruvate, I say to my students, then I don't expect you to rote learn chemical formulae either. Sure, you should know that water is H_2O, carbon dioxide is CO_2, and perhaps even that ethanol is C_2H_5OH. But, truly, memorizing formulae is for mugs (or for biochemistry students who go dewy eyed for this stuff).[1]

Being able to predict what a formula might say about the properties of that substance is a different thing altogether: it is certainly helpful to forecast what might be acidic, might inhibit foam, and so on. But

---

[1] As a biochemistry undergraduate at the University of Hull, I used to head to the pub, order my pint, and then peel apart the drip mat to expose the white insides, on which I would draw out the Embden–Meyerhof–Parnas pathway, the Krebs cycle, and other metabolic routes. I was usually alone—at least after a few minutes of this.

the starting point to the thought process should be the formula on a piece of paper or a computer screen, not something dredged up from the deepest little grey cell.

And so, as we embark on a journey through the molecules that are responsible for beer flavor, I do not intend to bombard the reader with formulae or any other complex biochemistry. The topic is complex enough without that. There are plenty of references where this information can be obtained in Appendix 3.

Bitterness

The bitterness of beer is almost entirely owing to molecules derived from the resin fraction of hops. There has been a suggestion that hydrophobic amino acids such as leucine or valine might contribute to bitterness, as might some of the polyphenols, just as grape tannins can afford a bitter character to some wines. I contend, however, that the contribution of amino acids or polyphenols can only be minor when compared with the iso-α-acids.

Focusing on the hop resins, although there are a number of fractions within the resin portfolio in the lupulin glands of hops, realistically we really only need to worry about the α-acids, of which there are three: humulone, cohumulone, and adhumulone. These are neither particularly soluble nor bitter, but if their structure is rearranged in a chemical reaction called isomerization, they are converted into more soluble and bitter forms, the iso-α-acids. Each of the α-acids is converted into two quite distinct iso-α-acids, which differ in the shape of the molecule. They are called the *cis* form and the *trans* form. The significance is that the six different iso-α-acids have different properties, including different bitterness intensities and (some would have it) *qualities* of bitterness, although that remains a judgment call.

Paul Hughes showed that isocohumulones are less bitter than isohumulones and that for any given iso-α-acid, the *cis* isomer is more bitter than the *trans* version. So, for a precise control of bitterness intensity, it is relevant to specify the hop variety, because different varieties have different levels of the three α-acids, and one should also be mindful of the mode of isomerization. Traditional boiling will tend to give a ratio of approximately two-thirds *trans* to one-third *cis*, whereas some of the preisomerized commercial preparations may have an increased proportion of the *cis* isomer and, therefore, at any given bitterness unit level (see chapter 6) will give a more intense bitterness.

Even more bitter, molecule for molecule, are the isomerized preparations that are reduced (typically through the addition of four hydrogen atoms) to protect against skunking. Thus, to get a given perceived bitterness, it is necessary to add less of these materials than would be the addition rate for, say, hop pellets if they were to be used.

Sourness

For sourness, read acidity. The lower the pH of a beer, the more sour it will be. In turn, the pH is influenced by a number of factors:

- The darker the malt, the lower will be the pH (so, for example, darker ales tend to have lower pHs than paler lagers).
- The higher the calcium level in the brew, the lower will be the pH.
- The higher the bicarbonate level in the water, the higher will be the pH.
- The more vigorous and extensive the fermentation, the lower will be the pH.
- The more buffering potential in the grist, the higher will be the pH, because buffers are materials that tend to "hold pH." And so grist bills that are rich in malt will tend to have higher pHs than brews from grists featuring increased levels of sugars and syrups.
- If bacteria such as lactic acid bacteria form a part of the recipe (as with lambic beers), the pH will be lower.
- Beers fermented at high gravity tend to have higher pHs than do equivalent beers brewed at "sales gravity."

As well as sourness, it has been suggested that pH impacts other flavor characteristics. It is said that at pHs lower than 4, beers become more *sharp*, with an increased *drying* character in the aftertaste and an increased perceived *bitterness*. At pHs less than 3.7, there might be a *metallic* afterpalate, whereas at pHs greater than 4.4, *soapy* and *caustic* notes have been reported, as well as *mouthcoating, biscuit*, and *toast*.

Sweetness

Sweetness derives from any sugars that survive fermentation or that are added as "primings" to the finished beer once yeast has been removed. In most fermentations, pretty much all of the sugars that yeast can use will be removed. The nonfermentable carbohydrates do not deliver any significant sweetness, although they are claimed to afford body (see more on this point later).

Thus, if the sweetness of a beer needs to be increased, perhaps to balance the sourness and bitterness, then the logical approach is to add priming sugar. As can be seen in Table 5-1, sucrose (the same sugar you add to your coffee) is two to three times sweeter than maltose. It has been argued by some that if you want to deliver an enhanced mouthfeel to a beer for a given amount of sweetness, then the best approach is to use a much less sweet sugar that would need to be added in much higher quantities. More molecules mean more lusciousness. Historically, the sugar of choice is the milk sugar lactose, which is added prior to fermentation because yeast cannot use it. There is a longstanding history of its use in products logically named "milk stouts." Lactose has only one-fifth the sweetness of sucrose.

TABLE 5-1.

The Relative Sweetness of Different Sugars[a]

Sugar	Relative Sweetness
Glucose	0.7–0.8
Maltose	0.3–0.5
Lactose	0.2
Fructose	1.1–1.2
Sucrose	1.0

[a] Based on Bamforth (2006).

Salt

Saltiness is not a trait that many think of when it comes to beer. However, the entities that deliver the classic salty taste (sodium and to a lesser extent potassium) are, of course, present in all beers. For this reason, they need to be regulated and will be influenced by the grist, by any additions made in the process, and especially by the water used in the brewery.

In this category perhaps we should also consider other flavor notes delivered by the diverse inorganic salts that are present in beer, the levels of which will also be influenced by raw materials (especially water) and additions.

Many a brewer is convinced about the importance of sulfate and chloride. The former is said to afford dryness, whereas chloride gives palate fullness and "mellowness" (whatever that is).

Hoppy

The aroma that arises from the essential oils of hops is extremely difficult to tie down to a few specific chemical components. Although the specific note associated with some of the chemical species is known (Table 5-2), the aroma delivered is never owing to just one or even to a few types of molecules. There may be more than 300 different species in the oil fraction, and although not all of them will make an impact, it certainly makes for an exceedingly complex scenario. For this reason, hop aroma is controlled on the basis of three factors:

- hop variety,
- time of addition, and
- amount added.

TABLE 5-2.

Some Components from the Essential Oil of Hops and Their Aroma[a]

Compound	Aroma
Noncitrusy compounds	
2,5,5-Trimethyl-2, 6-heptadien-ol	Wormwood oil, terpene
cis-2,6-Dimethyl-2, 6-octadiene	
Ethyl isovalerate	Fruity, apple
Citronellene	
2,7-Dimethyl-2,7-octadiene	
β-Myrcene	Woody, vegetative, citrus, fruity with tropical mango and slight leafy minty nuances
Linalool	sweet, floral
Methyl geranate	Waxy, green, fruity, flower

[a] Courtesy of Thomas Shellhammer, Oregon State University.

continued

TABLE 5-2. continued

Some Components from the Essential Oil of Hops and Their Aroma[a]

Compound	Aroma
Humulene	Woody
Ethyl *trans*-4-decenoate	Fruity, pear-like, apple-like
α-Terpinolene	
δ-Cadinene	
β-Damascenone	Berry-like
Geranyl acetate	Sweet fruity, possible synergy
β-Ionone	Violets, floral
Caryophyllene oxide	Woody
γ-Nonalactone	Tropical enhancer
Viridiflorol	Sweet, green, herbal, fruity, tropical, minty
Cubenol	Spicy
Ethyl cinnamate (cinnamon)	Cinnamon
Caryophyllene	Woody
α-Selinene	Herbal
τ-Cadinol	Earthy, balmy
Guaiene	Woody, peppery, balsam
σ-Cadinol	Herbal
α-Eudesmol	Not an odor-active isomer
β-Eudesmol	Woody, green
α-Cadinol	Herbal, woody
Geranyl linalool	Mild floral balsam
β-Selinene	Herbal
δ-Dodecalactone	Tropical
Citrusy compounds	
2-Methyl-2-penten-1-ol	Green apple, orange fruit
Ocimene	Warm, floral, herb, flower, sweet
β-Farnesene	Woody citrus, sweet
β-Citronellal	
α-Farnesene	Woody sweet, used to enhance citrus

continued

TABLE 5-2. continued

Some Components from the Essential Oil of Hops and Their Aroma[a]

Compound	Aroma
Nerol	Natural sweetness, citrus enhancer
β-Citronellol	Citronella oil, rose leaf, oily petal
Geraniol	Sweet flowery, citrus enhancer
Neral/citral	Strong citrus
Nerolidol	Fruity, flowery
(E,Z)α-Farnesene	A woody, green vegetative odor with a lavender background, definite citrus synergy
β-Farnesol	Citrus, herbaceous

In just the same way that grape varietals can be distinguished according to characteristic aromas, so it is for hops, although this concept is far less explored. One of the reasons for this paucity is that there can be a great divergence between what a hop smells like when it is rubbed between the palms and what the aroma is when the hop is used to late hop or dry hop a beer (of which more momentarily). However, it behooves the brewer and hop supplier to be able to articulate the nature of hop aroma, as it undoubtedly gives some indication of the character delivered to a beer, at least by dry hopping. Table 5-3 illustrates data generated in our studies that we believe take us further forward in the understanding of how different hops can be differentiated and described according to their "nose."

Hop aroma can be delivered in two ways: either by adding a proportion of hops later into the kettle boil (or hot wort receiver) or by adding hops to the finished beer. The former is known as late hopping and is historically associated with lager brewing, notably the pilsners. The latter is referred to as dry hopping and is classically a part of the brewing of ales, notably cask-conditioned bitters in the United Kingdom. Dry hopping affords a much more complex hop character, as there is the lowest degree of loss of oil components. These molecules are volatile and tend to be purged readily, especially in wort boiling. If all the hop material is added at the start of boiling, the aroma constituents are

TABLE 5-3.

Mean Scores (Scale 0–5) for Significant Flavors Detected in Whole Cone Hops[a]

Hop Variety	Pine-Sol	Garlic	Cheesy	Hay	Orange	Raisin
Apollo	1.5	4.3	2.8	1.8	1.2	0.8
Bravo	2.2	2.8	2.0	1.6	2.6	1.3
Cascade	1.9	2.5	1.7	2.4	2.3	1.2
Delta	1.8	1.6	1.8	2.7	1.8	1.4
Hallertau	1.2	2.5	2.3	3.1	1.5	1.5
Herkules	1.6	4.0	3.6	1.6	1.9	1.2
Opal	1.2	3.0	2.6	2.6	1.6	0.9
Saaz	1.1	0.7	0.8	4.2	1.2	1.9
Saphir	1.0	2.3	2.2	2.8	1.6	1.6
Smaragd	1.0	3.9	4.4	1.8	1.1	1.1
Summit	1.9	4.0	2.8	1.6	1.8	0.8
Tradition	1.1	1.6	1.7	3.4	1.1	1.5
Willamette	1.7	2.3	2.5	3.1	1.9	1.4
	Grapefruit	Green Tea	Wet Wood	Lemon/Lime	Herbal	Mint
Apollo	2.8	2.0	1.0	2.3	2.1	1.4
Bravo	3.3	2.6	0.7	2.6	1.3	1.5
Cascade	2.4	2.6	0.8	2.1	1.2	1.2
Delta	2.2	3.1	0.9	1.7	1.2	1.1
Hallertau	1.7	3.0	1.5	1.3	1.4	0.9
Herkules	1.9	2.3	1.0	1.8	1.7	1.4
Opal	1.9	2.6	1.5	1.2	1.6	1.0
Saaz	1.0	4.0	2.2	0.7	1.5	1.1
Saphir	1.5	3.1	1.6	1.1	1.5	1.0
Smaragd	1.4	2.5	1.1	1.2	2.1	0.9
Summit	3.1	2.1	1.0	1.7	2.1	1.0
Tradition	1.3	3.2	1.3	0.9	1.4	1.0
Willamette	2.0	3.3	1.5	1.6	1.1	1.5

[a] Derived from Donaldson et al (2012).

essentially entirely lost, hence the late addition. In late hopping there is an additional complication in that some of the components are likely transformed by yeast, with an impact on flavor.

Malty

Just as for hop aroma, malt-derived character is also an extremely complex business, not easily reduced to one or even a few chemical species. There are, of course, diverse types of malt, including those differentiated according to the intensity of heating that has been afforded to the grain. The flavor notes associated with them are quite different.

When the term "malty" is employed to describe flavor, it usually refers to the character associated with the pale, lightly dried malts that not only feature in the aroma of beer but also in other foodstuffs such as breakfast cereals, breads, and cookies. Think malted milk balls. It is understood that 3- and 2-methylbutanal, maltol, and ethylmethylpyrazines are prime determinants of this type of character, but again (just as for hops) it is probably more useful to define and control malt character on the basis of controlling barley variety, the way it is steeped and germinated, and especially the way it is kilned.

Nigel Davies and his colleagues did develop a lexicon of malt aroma (Table 5-4) and concluded that the precise malt house conditions impacted flavor delivery. For example, the extent of air recirculation on the kiln had a profound effect: ostensibly the same malt, fulfilling all the target specifications, could display different flavors depending on the extent to which air had been recirculated.

Of course, the chemistry of the more intensely kilned malts is even more complex than that of the pale malts, but the same considerations in terms of flavor apply.

There is as much application of art and experience as there is science in the control of both hop- and malt-derived aroma.

TABLE 5-4.

Flavor Descriptors for Malt[a]

Note	Thesaurus
Cereal	Cookie, biscuit, hay, muesli, pastry
Sweet	Honey
Burnt	Toast, roast
Nutty (green)	Bean sprout, cauliflower, grassy, green pea, seaweed
Nutty (roast)	Chestnut, peanut, walnut, Brazil nut
Sulfury	Cooked vegetable, dimethyl sulfide
Harsh	Acidic, sour, sharp
Toffee	Vanilla
Caramel	Cream soda
Coffee	Espresso
Chocolate	Dark chocolate
Treacle	Treacle toffee
Smoky	Bonfire, wood fire, peaty
Phenolic	Spicy, medicinal, herbal
Fruity	Fruit jam, banana, citrus, fruitcake
Bitter	Quinine
Astringent	Mouth puckering
Other	Cardboard, earthy, damp paper
Linger	Duration and intensity of aftertaste

[a] Derived from Murray et al (1999).

Vicinal Diketones

There are two significant vicinal diketones (VDKs) in beer: diacetyl and pentanedione. The first of these has a characteristic butterscotch or popcorn aroma, and the second is variously described as honey, butter, caramel, or just plain sweet. The flavor threshold[2] of pentanedione is some 10 times higher than that of diacetyl, making the latter the one that concerns brewers more, but pentanedione cannot be ignored.

Most brewers would argue that VDKs are merely negative and should be eliminated; however, it can be argued that their presence is important to the flavor of some beers, for instance, some darker ales. Diacetyl is also deliberately present in some Czech lagers.

Both VDKs arise from precursors that leak out of the yeast cell (Fig. 5-1). These break down spontaneously in the fermenting wort. However, yeast will progressively scavenge and remove them, ultimately lowering their levels to below the flavor threshold.

The level at which they are detected (i.e., their flavor threshold) depends on the beer. Essentially, the less intensely flavored the beer, the lower the level that needs to be attained if they are not going to be detectable. And so a fairly fully flavored pale lager may have a flavor threshold for diacetyl of 0.1 ppm, but more gently flavored lagers may need diacetyl levels to be taken to as low as 0.02 ppm.

Of prime importance are the health and amount of the yeast cells. Fundamentally, the removal of the VDKs during or at the end of fermentation (the latter is sometimes known as warm conditioning) is key to regulation of this critical flavor component.

---

[2] Flavor threshold is the concentration at which a substance becomes detectable in a drink. The more potent the flavor substance, the lower the flavor threshold is. When tested by adding a substance to water, the threshold tends to be lower than when the substance is added in controlled amounts to beer, because of masking effects. The determination of flavor thresholds is not easy. Furthermore, in a complex matrix such as beer you can have interacting effects. For example, if there are several substances all with similar structures—and, therefore, similar flavors because they all interact with the same detection mechanism in the nose and mouth—then even if they are all at low levels well below their flavor thresholds, cumulatively they can be detectable by the senses. Another complication is that one flavor may block another by interacting with its detection system in ways that are not entirely understood. Thus, phenylethanol and phenylethyl acetate were shown to interfere with the perception of dimethyl sulfide.

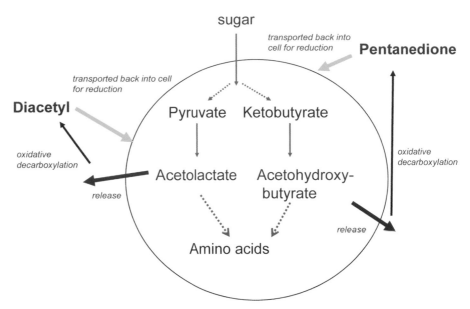

Fig. 5-1. Production of the vicinal diketones diacetyl and pentanedione. The circle represents a yeast cell. Dotted lines mean that there are several successive reactions here.

Esters

Whereas there are only two significant VDKs in beer, there are several esters with a range of associated aromas (Table 5-5).

An ester is a substance made from an alcohol and a carboxylic acid. The most significant ester in beer is usually isoamyl acetate, on

TABLE 5-5.

The Flavor of Some Esters

Ester	Flavor
Isoamyl acetate	Banana, bubble gum
Ethyl acetate	Pear drops, nail polish
Ethyl octanoate	Apple, fruity
Ethyl butyrate	Papaya, mango, canned pineapple
Ethyl hexanoate	Apple, aniseed (at very high levels)
Phenylethyl acetate	Rose, honey
Ethyl caprylate	Apple, sweet, fruity

42

account of its relatively low flavor threshold and presence at levels in excess of that threshold. As the name implies, it is made from the reaction of isoamyl alcohol and acetic acid (more specifically an activated form of acetic acid called acetyl coenzyme A). A notable feature of the esters is that they tend to be much more potent aromawise than their building blocks. Thus, the flavor threshold of isoamyl acetate is around 1 mg/L, whereas that of isoamyl alcohol is approximately 50 mg/L and that of acetic acid is 2,175 mg/L.

Like the VDKs, the esters are products of yeast metabolism. The yeast makes both alcohols and acids (discussed momentarily) and, in turn, links them together as esters. The metabolism is far from simple, but if we are to make some generalizations, it would be that yeast strain is extremely important and, at least as important, anything that tends to suppress yeast growth tends to increase the level of esters (and vice versa) (Fig. 5-2).

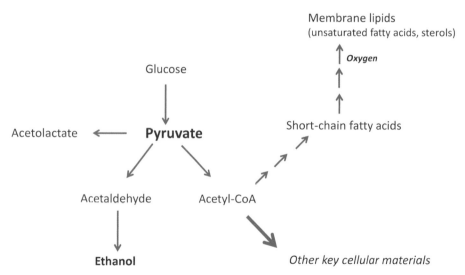

Fig. 5-2. Pyruvate is a key intermediary metabolite produced from the breakdown of wort sugars. It can, of course, be converted via acetaldehyde to ethanol (for which we are eternally grateful). Or it can be transformed into acetolactate for amino acid synthesis (see earlier). Or it can be transformed into acetyl-coenzyme A (acetyl-CoA, a sort of high-power acetic acid), which is the building block for many key cellular processes and structural materials. These include the long-chain unsaturated fatty acids and the sterols that make up membranes. The last stage in making those lipids involves oxygen. If there is insufficient oxygen, then the synthetic pathway halts, and there is a buildup of short-chain fatty acid CoA complexes and, in turn, of acetyl-CoA, which is then attached by a yeast enzyme onto alcohols such as ethanol and isoamyl alcohol to make esters.

Alcohols

Yeast produces a diversity of alcohols, of which the most prominent, of course, is ethanol (ethyl alcohol), in comparison with which all the others (collectively referred to as "higher alcohols") are in relatively small quantity (Table 5-6). Alcohols are produced by the yeast adding hydrogen atoms to aldehydes and ketones (cumulatively known as carbonyl compounds). In the case of ethanol, the relevant aldehyde is acetaldehyde (see the later section on carbonyl compounds).

In turn, the carbonyl compounds are derived in two possible ways (Fig. 5-3). They can arise as products of yeast metabolic pathways. This is how acetaldehyde arises at a late stage in the degradation of sugars. Alternatively, they can be produced from the amino acids that yeast assimilates from the wort. In this case, the first thing that the yeast does is take away the nitrogen-containing portion (the amino group) from the amino acid and replace it with a carbonyl group. And, as we have said, this group can then have hydrogen added to it to make an alcohol. The higher alcohols will tend to be produced in elevated amounts if the yeast is fed high amounts of amino acids. However, we will also see that insufficient amino acids result in increased levels of the higher alcohols.

TABLE 5-6.

The Flavor of Some Alcohols[a]

Alcohol	Perceived Character
Ethanol	Alcoholic
Propanol	Alcoholic
Isobutanol	Alcoholic
Isoamyl alcohol	Alcohol, banana, vinous
Tyrosol	Bitter
Phenylethanol	Roses, perfume

[a] From Bamforth (2006).

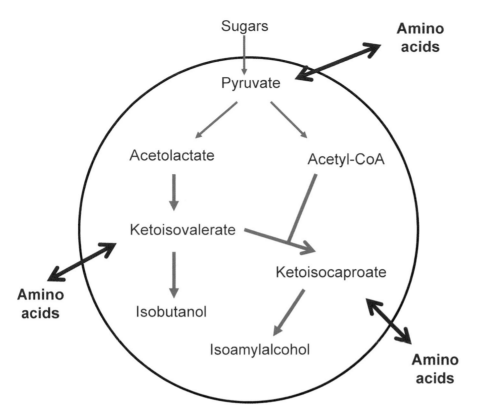

Fig. 5-3. Alcohols are either made through the metabolism of carbohydrates leading to amino acid synthesis or from an excess of amino acids present in the wort. If there is too little free amino nitrogen in the wort, then the yeast cannot complete the final stage in amino acid synthesis (adding the N atom), and the metabolites are channeled into alcohol production. If there is too much N (i.e., amino acids) in the wort, then the excess is converted into alcohols. The circle represents a yeast cell.

Acids

The acids we speak of here are the carboxylic acids. A range of these are intermediates in the metabolic pathways by which yeast deals with the sugars in wort, and among them are pyruvic acid, citric acid, and α-ketoglutaric acid. Yeast will also produce acetic acid, albeit in much lower quantities than do the acetic acid bacteria that can contaminate beer under conditions in which there can be a significant availability of oxygen, for example, in the dispensing of draft beer.

TABLE 5-7.

The Flavor of Some Fatty Acids[a]

Fatty Acid	Perceived Character
Acetic	Vinegar
Propionic	Acidic, milky
Butyric	Cheesy
3-Methyl butyric	Sweaty
Caproic	Vegetable oil
Caprylic	Goaty
Phenyl acetic	Honey

[a] From Bamforth (2006).

A range of short-chain fatty acids (Table 5-7) are also intermediates in the production by yeast of the lipids that make up its membranes. If for some reason the yeast is unable to complete the synthesis of those lipids, then there tends to be a buildup in the level of these short-chain fatty acids, which are usually associated with undesirable flavors such as *wet dog* and *goaty*. It needs to be borne in mind that a given aroma perception in beer—*wet dog* being a good example—can actually be owing to a series of substances of different types rather than being absolutely linked to a single chemical.

Sulfur-Containing Substances

Some of the most potent aroma compounds in beer contain the sulfur atom (Table 5-8).

The sulfur can come from two sources. The first is inorganic sulfur, notably sulfate in the water supply (think hard water) or sulfite, including some that might be added directly as an antioxidant (metabisulfite) or as a preservative (e.g., in isinglass finings). The second source of sulfur is organic sulfur, notably amino acids that contain sulfur, namely, cysteine and methionine. Thus, the sulfur available to yeast is not only these two amino acids present in the wort but also any inorganic sulfur in the wort that the yeast can then use (through metabolic routes) to make sulfur-containing amino acids and other substances.

TABLE 5-8.

The Flavor of Some Sulfur-Containing Substances[a]

Sulfur-Containing Compound	Perceived Character
Hydrogen sulfide	Rotten eggs
Sulfur dioxide	Burnt matches
Methyl mercaptan	Rotting vegetables
Ethyl mercaptan	Rotting vegetables
Propyl mercaptan	Onion
Dimethyl sulfide	Sweet corn
Dimethyl disulfide	Rotting vegetables
Dimethyl trisulfide	Rotting vegetables, onion
Methyl thioacetate	Cooked cabbage
Diethyl sulfide	Cooked vegetables, garlic
Methional	Cooked potato
3-Methyl-2-butene-1-thiol	Lightstruck, skunky

[a] From Bamforth (2006).

However, not all sulfur containing flavor-active substances arise from yeast metabolism. Notable among these is 3-methyl-2-butene-1-thiol (MBT), which is the main component of the skunky character of lightstruck beer. This molecule develops from the breaking off of a chunk of the iso-α-acids (the bitter compounds) derived from hops. This broken off entity reacts with traces of sulfur-containing materials in the beer (nobody is absolutely certain which substances these are) to make MBT. The process is started by light, which is captured by a vitamin (riboflavin) in the beer and handed off to the iso-α-acids. This is what triggers the shearing off of the side arm.

Most people would consider hydrogen sulfide (H_2S, *rotten egg*) to be an undesirable feature of beer aroma; however, that is not universally the case. Traditional ales from Burton-on-Trent in England display a character that has come to be known even in polite circles as the "Burton snatch." If you pull a fresh pint of such a beer, it displays a distinct egginess that gradually diminishes to reveal the dry hop character. It arises by the action of yeast adding hydrogen to the sulfate, of which there are huge quantities in the exceptionally hard waters of the

Midlands town. If beer brewed from water containing much less sulfate shows an H_2S note, then it is symptomatic of a less than fully vigorous fermentation. If a fermentation proceeds vigorously, with ample carbon dioxide evolution, then the egginess should be dissipated.

Perhaps the most extensively studied sulfur-containing substance is dimethyl sulfide (DMS), which is usually said to afford a *canned corn* note. It was shown in the 1970s to be a prime feature of many Germanic lager-style beers, although it is generally considered in that nation to be an off flavor. It certainly seems to attract a divergence of opinion, from those who find its presence to be reprehensible through to those who have substantial amounts in their brands.[3] Ultimately, it all arises from an amino acid derivative in malted barley called *S*-methylmethionine (SMM) and, because SMM is located in the embryo, the more extensive the germination of the grain, the more SMM will develop. It is an extremely heat-sensitive molecule and, accordingly, the more vigorous the kilning, the more substantial will be the loss of SMM. It breaks down to DMS, which is lost with the flue gases. Thus, pale ale malts tend to contain less SMM ("DMS potential") than do the lighter dried malts, such as pilsner malts. The temperatures are high enough in wort boiling for the SMM extracted from malt in mashing to be broken down to DMS and, provided the conditions are turbulent, the DMS will be driven off. However, in the hot wort stand (whirlpool), it is hot enough for any remaining SMM to be broken down but insufficiently turbulent for the

---

[3] I vividly recall one disagreement over dimethyl sulfide (DMS) levels. There was little love lost between the brewery in Glasgow that was under the company umbrella and the headquarters in Burton. So I was on a hiding to nothing when dispatched to Scotland to tell them that they must raise their DMS levels from 30 μg/L (at which they were running) to 50 μg/L (which was the group standard for the lager in question). I was told in no uncertain terms that the perception of DMS was identical in both beers, that it "came through" in their beer at the lower level, and that if it was increased it would be objectionable. They said my time would be better spent finding out why that was rather than wasting their time with my nonsense. My colleague Roy Parsons duly showed that, indeed, there was a masking of DMS aroma by phenylethanol and phenylethyl acetate and that both of these were present at significantly lower levels in the Scottish version. But the payoff was this: those molecules were at lower levels because the Scots were not following company practice and were fermenting the beer at a temperature 2°C lower than the edict. They told me that they did not feel inclined to change.

DMS to be lost. Accordingly, as a rule of thumb, if you seek to avoid DMS, then go for less well-modified malt that is highly dried, and then combine a vigorous long boil with a short time in the whirlpool. The other extreme (for a high DMS level) would be lightly dried but well-modified malt with a relatively short boil and a long whirlpool stand. The situation is actually more complicated than this. In fermentation, there is substantial loss of DMS, which is stripped off with the CO_2. There will be more DMS loss in, say, an open square fermenter than a large cylindroconical fermenter. However, there is also DMS production in the fermentation, through the action of yeast adding hydrogen to dimethyl sulfoxide (DMSO), which also originates in the embryo of malt from the degradation of SMM. Yeast is not especially efficient in this process, but nonetheless some claim that the majority of the DMS in their beers originates from this reaction. Actually, wort spoilage bacteria such as *Obesumbacterium* spp. are much more adept at handling DMSO and will convert all of it to DMS in short order.

Methyl thioacetate (flavor) is produced by yeast using the same enzyme that makes the esters that we spoke of earlier. And so, if there are substantial quantities of methanethiol present, they can be converted into the thioester by reaction with acetic acid.

Surprisingly, less is known about the other sulfur-containing flavor substances and their origins, and control strategies still warrant attention.

Carbonyl Compounds

We have already encountered some of these (for example, 3- and 2-methylbutanal) when we spoke of malt flavor. Carbonyl substances as a whole, however, will be the focus of the next volume in this series, as they are at the heart of flavor instability.

Here we will address just one—namely, acetaldehyde—which has the aroma of *green apple*. It is produced by yeast in the later stages of sugar degradation and is the immediate precursor of ethanol. If it remains in any significant quantity in beer, it is likely a sign of poorly performing yeast. However, even with healthy and vigorously fermenting yeast, the blandest beers may need a somewhat prolonged conditioning time to eradicate the last traces of this molecule. A second source of acetaldehyde is spoilage bacteria, notably *Zymomonas* spp.

Phenolics

Although some believe that polyphenols contribute to astringency and mouthfeel in beer, just as they do in red wine and hard cider, in reality their levels are usually quite low in comparison to those other drinks, so this is unlikely to be the case. However, some molecules containing the phenol group can make a real contribution to beer flavor. The most significant of these is 4-vinylguiaicol, which has the aroma of *clove*. It is produced by organisms that are able to remove carbon dioxide from ferulic acid, which is a component of the cell walls of cereals and is extracted in mashing. Most brewing yeasts do not have the gene that codes for the enzyme that performs this reaction, but the ale yeasts used to make hefeweissen do, hence the presence of a clove-like note as an indicator that authentic hefeweissen yeast has been used. Diverse nonbrewing yeast strains do possess this ability.

Miscellaneous Off-Flavors

Grainy/Astringent

These characteristics are associated with materials (notably tannic substances) that are associated with the husk. Thus, more agitation in malt extraction and greater efforts to pull out the last remnants of extract during wort separation, especially if the pH is allowed to rise, will lead to a greater instance of graininess. There may be a tendency for wet milling to lead to increased grainy character, and (from personal experience) a less than fully vigorous rolling boil also seems to lead to more carryover of a grainy note.

Musty

Musty notes in beer may suggest microbial problems—perhaps *Brettanomyces* spp.—or may be linked to a problem with some materials employed in the layering of empty containers prior to filling with cork closures (think "corked" in wine).

Antiseptic/Plastic/Hospital-like

Most likely this off-flavor reflects a problem with the water, specifically the presence of chlorinated materials.

Cheesy

Most prominently, this note can arise from badly stored hops. The bitter acids degrade into cheesy substances, so always store hops air tight and cold.

Mouthfeel

Gus, my boss, had a thing about the mouthfeel of beer. He told me one day that it was high time I got to grips with the texture of beer.

"Texture?" I said. "But beer is wet."

"I know," he replied, "but there's wet and there's wet."

And I guess he was right: compare how a low-carbohydrate lager and a draft stout feel in the mouth as you slosh them about.

Ronald Jowitt defined mouthfeel as "those textural attributes of a food or beverage responsible for producing characteristic tactile sensations on the surfaces of the oral cavity."

The flavor wheel suggests the following ways to describe mouthfeel: *warming, carbonation (flat, gassy), powdery, astringent, metallic,* and *mouthcoating.* Table 5-9 lists the relationship between some of these characteristics and the chemical species that are probably responsible for them.

TABLE 5-9.

Mouthfeel Terms and Contributing Compounds

Term	Compound
Astringent	Organic acids
Drying	Lactic acid, ethanol
Warming	Ethanol
Mouthcoating	Salts (e.g., sodium chloride and sodium sulfate)
Liveliness	Carbon dioxide

John Clapperton, a main driving force behind the flavor wheel, suggested that individual compounds impact perceived mouthfeel characteristics; for example, amounts of diacetyl that would be definitely too high from a flavor perspective (0.6 ppm) are detected as mouthcoating and body.

Susan Langstaff, pursuing her Ph.D. at the University of California, Davis, back in the early 1990s, proposed that the beer flavor wheel should be modified and divided into three parts: *carbonation, fullness,* and *afterfeel.* Table 5-10 illustrates the subterms within each of these.

TABLE 5-10.

Nomenclature for Mouthfeel[a]

Mouthfeel Term	Mouthfeel Subterm
Carbonation	Total carbon dioxide
Foam volume	
Bubble size	
Sting	
Fullness	Density
Viscosity	
Afterfeel	Astringency
Stickiness	
Oily mouthcoat	

[a] Derived from Langstaff and Lewis (1993).

The foam clearly can have an impact—imagine a stout straight from the tap in Ireland featuring a deep head of small bubbles, with substantial liquid hold-up. Nitrogen gas obviously is key to this superbly stable foam, but I am not convinced that the remarkable foam is the sole reason why the use of N_2 (as little as 20–30 mg/L) can have such a huge impact on mouthfeel in making the liquid almost velvety smooth to the palate. I am not sure that anyone has yet answered that question.

The other major component responsible for foaming is, of course, carbon dioxide. It is the source of the tingle in beer, the bite, the sting. Nitrogenated beers generally contain less CO_2 than the norm, which is one reason for their smoother palate (although surely not the only one, because cask ales devoid of nitrogen are much less smooth than nitrokegs). We are *feeling* the irritation from the CO_2, which is surely the biggest manifestation of mouthfeel in a beer.

Some have suggested that organic acids may be important for mouthfeel—think what your mouth feels like after eating rhubarb, an effect owing to oxalic acid. Others suggest polyphenols with their astringency. In either case, the levels that would be needed in beer to impact mouthfeel are far higher than is normally seen.

Alcohol, of course, provides a warming influence, which means that products containing more alcohol, such as barley wines, tend to have a fuller palate feel. (Hot spices such as chili have the same impact.)

Proteins, polypeptides, β-glucans, glycerol, and chloride have all been touted for their supposed impact on mouthfeel, but at their levels in most beers there can be no reality of their individual contribution. More than any other substance, dextrins have been championed for superior mouthfeel. Susan Langstaff showed that more than 50 g/L of dextrins would need to be added to a superattenuated beer to have any impact on mouthfeel, a level considerably higher than found in the vast majority of beers.

Perhaps it is nothing more than the sheer quantity of everything in a beer that really matters: in other words, the greater the number of all molecules dissolved in the beer, the greater will be the overall impact on physical phenomena such as viscosity, shown by Langstaff to be a key parameter. Perhaps not as viscous as honey—and you know what that feels like in the mouth!—but surely a beer with extremely high original extract will register more resistance to swirling in the mouth than one that is far lighter.

Chapter 5

The Molecules of Flavor and How They Find Their Way into Beer

Quantifying Flavor

I will never forget the time I pitched up in the 1990s at a brewery not far from Birmingham in England. Having toured the compact operation, I retired with the owner/brewmaster to a nearby pub, where two pints of the nectar that was their best bitter were placed before us. I took a sip.

"Hmm, that's quite bitter," I offered.

"Yes it is," agreed my host.

"What is the bitterness?" I asked.

"Well, the last time we measured it, it was 35."

"When was that?"

"1954."

He was unfazed. His concept of quality control involved selection of the specified hop variety, knowledge of its α-acid content, specifying the boiling conditions, and tweaking according to taste—his taste, as the person who knew more about that beer than anyone else on the planet.

And that's okay. It works for anyone who knows what they are doing and who cares about doing it right (always presupposing that they are decent tasters).

Thus, the laboratory of many a brewer is stocked fairly minimally. Their most sensitive analytical instrumentation is portable, namely, their nose, mouth, and eyes. Ears, too, sometimes, considering pumps and the damage that they might cause. It works.

Even in the most sophisticated of breweries, I still contend that the sensory team (see chapter 4) is more important than the analytical lab when it comes to controlling the taste and smell of the beer. Having said that, there is inevitably a call for analytical techniques, at the very least to back up the sensory work and to serve in the event of debate, for example, between a brand owner and franchisee who disagree on whether a note is or is not present in a product. For brewers intent on the closest possible batch-to-batch control, making quantitative measurements is always important. Remember, though, that at most a brewer measures precious few of the hundreds, even thousands, of molecules that potentially might contribute to beer flavor.

Thinking back to my time as a quality assurance manager, the only flavorsome substances we measured on every batch were alcohol, carbon dioxide, total VDKs (read on for what I mean by that), bitterness units, and for our lagers, DMS (because we were obsessed with the stuff). Because pH also confirmed that the sourness was in the correct ballpark, we can add that to the list.

Other entities (for example, the esters) were surveyed monthly. Most volatiles were never measured.

As we have seen in chapter 4, we placed great store on the formal and informal tasting regimes. This, of course, was on the back of detailed specifications for the raw materials and for all processes.

I know of one megacompany that pretty much measured everything for a very straightforward reason: the top man made a habit of demanding a number at any time of the day or night, and woe betide if it was not forthcoming.

I preach the middle way: some analytical information but not overkill. So how do we make some of these measurements? However, keep in mind one of my golden rules: we should foist measurements whenever possible onto others, such as suppliers.

Controlling Bitterness

There are two primary relevant measures: the α-acid content of the hop product (ASBC Hops-6) and the iso-α-acid level in the beer (ASBC Beer-23). The former should be provided by the supplier and will most likely have been generated through a spectrophotometric procedure involving the measurement of ultraviolet light absorption at three wavelengths. If the hop product is preisomerized extract for downstream addition, then rather than α-acid, the numbers will be quantifying iso-α-acids.

Beer (or wort) bitterness can be ascertained in two ways: through spectrophotometry or chromatography. The former can be performed with fairly straightforward techniques and relatively inexpensive equipment. Indeed, a relatively inexpensive spectrophotometer can be used to make various measurements, as we will see. The chromatographic approach involves high-performance liquid chromatography (HPLC) and is beyond the scope of most basic laboratories. Again, though, HPLC can be employed to make other measurements, such as sugars and polyphenols (basically, anything that is nonvolatile).[1]

In my experience, the spectrophotometric method—in which the bitter compounds are extracted in a solvent, the absorbance of UV light at 275 nm is measured, and this value is multiplied by 50 to get International Bitterness Units (IBU)—is perfectly adequate for most instances when seeking to measure bitterness. Back in 1989, Roy Cope, Kim Butcher, and I looked at the spectrophotometric and HPLC methods and found that neither gave an ideal representation of bitterness as scored by a flavor panel (Figs. 6-1 and 6-2). However, when we plotted the data from the two instrumental techniques against one another, we found a pretty decent correlation (Fig. 6-3). There was a slight intercept on the *x* axis, which represents those materials that had a degree of absorbance in the UV but were not bitterness compounds.

In other words, measuring bitterness by the spectrophotometric method was perfectly adequate. Some would argue about the quality of bitterness, for example, arising from different proportions of the various α-acids that are transformed into iso-α-acids differing in perceived bitterness (see chapter 5). Probably the most significant instance when this becomes relevant is when using preisomerized extracts. As we saw in chapter 5, these preparations tend to have a balance of isomers that

---

[1] A volatile substance is one that has a tendency to leave the beer and go into the headspace (the gas above the beer that your nose encounters as you drink). Thus, volatiles are primarily detected by the nose. They partition into the headspace because they have relatively low boiling points. Nonvolatile substances are those with relatively high boiling points that tend to remain in the beer and not go into the headspace. They are therefore detected on the tongue for the most part.

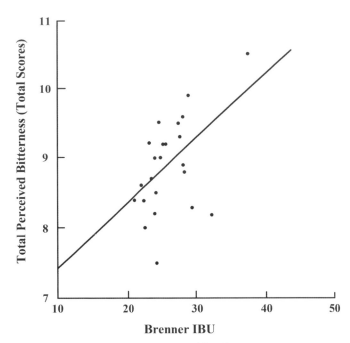

Fig. 6-1. Bitterness as measured by the Brenner spectrophotometric method versus that perceived by a sensory panel, as reported in Bamforth et al (1989).

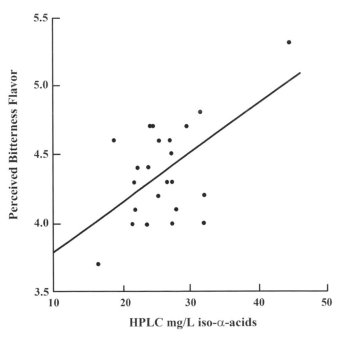

Fig. 6-2. Bitterness as measured by high-performance liquid chromatography (HPLC) versus that perceived by a sensory panel, as reported in Bamforth et al (1989).

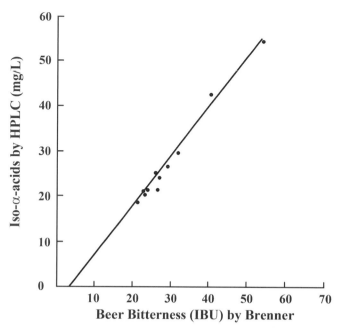

Fig. 6-3. A comparison of two instrumental methods for measuring bitterness. The Brenner spectrophotometric method is adequate, and the equipment required is more common than that for high-performance liquid chromatography (HPLC), as reported in Bamforth et al (1989).

is significantly bitterer than the balance obtained by conventional wort boiling. For this reason, the multiplier in the IBU calculation is usually increased from 50 to 70. The increase in bitterness proportional to the amount of isomerized material added is especially significant when using the reduced preparations tetra and hexa.

At the end of the day, it is up to the brewer to decide how much useful information they are getting from the bitterness measurement and to establish for a given mode of hopping what the correct IBU specification is brand by brand to achieve the bitterness perception that sits comfortably with them.

Sourness

Practically the only significant measure that needs to be made is pH (ASBC Beer-9), for which purpose a simple pH meter (properly calibrated on a regular basis) is perfectly adequate. Remember, too, that the pH measured depends on temperature. As the temperature is lowered, the pH tends to rise. So you need to specify what the temperature should be at to measure the pH; usually it is 20°C (68°F).

Sweetness

Although HPLC and other methods can measure sugars (also known as sweetness, ASBC Beer-41), in most instances this parameter is probably not worth considering for routine measurement. The level of residual sugars that would impact sweetness is likely to be very low in a properly fermented beer, and by attention to gravities and issues of fermentability, the target residual gravity in relation to pitching gravity should afford all the necessary evidence for an absence of unfermented sugars (combination of ASBC Beer-4, 5, and 6). Regarding priming, then (as for so many other quality considerations in a brewery), the control should be through specifying addition rates of indicated sweeteners.

Salts

The inorganic ions in beer originate from grist materials, water, and any additions. Of these, the water and salt additions attract the most attention. Most brewers will source their water from a local supplier, as opposed to their own well, and should expect to receive a regular report of water composition. However, it may only be by request that they will obtain a full listing of all the cations and anions, because suppliers only need to supply those line items specified in the regulations for potable water (see Appendix 3). Ions are measured by a selection of chromatographic techniques, including ion chromatography and atomic absorption spectrophotometry (ASBC Beer-20, 36–39, and 43).

Hop Aroma

Alongside malt aroma, hop aroma is nigh on impossible at present to relate to analytical measurement. Currently, there is no simple way to correlate numbers generated by techniques such as gas chromatography (GC, which is employed to quantify volatile substances) with a given hop aroma—say, late hop character, or the aroma of Cascade or any other hop variety. In other words, you can't look at a chromatographic printout of oil components and say "Ah! Unmistakably Fuggles." Yet experts can rub Fuggles between their palms and correctly identify it every time.

Malt Aroma

The same considerations apply as for hop aroma.

Vicinal Diketones

Although it is possible to measure VDKs spectrophotometrically (ASBC Beer-25B and C), it is not a particularly reliable or sensitive method. It really does require GC to measure them properly (ASBC Beer-25E).

The only worthwhile measurement is total VDK. This parameter represents the absolute amount not only of diacetyl and pentanedione but also their precursors (see chapter 5). Remember, those precursors break down spontaneously to release VDK, with the yeast subsequently mopping up the VDK. But what happens if the entire precursor does not break down, for whatever reason? If you measure only the free VDKs and find they are low enough for your satisfaction, you may be tempted to remove the yeast and package the beer. But the precursors are still lingering, and they will go on to break down in the beer, which will develop a butterscotch/popcorn/honey aroma. So a responsible brewer measures total VDK by taking the sample, heating it up to force the breakdown of the two precursors to their VDKs, and then measuring the latter, which will represent the VDK in the beer as is, together with the precursors.

Measurement of Flavorsome Volatiles

The esters, higher alcohols, and sulfur-containing compounds—indeed, any volatile materials in the beer—can be measured by GC (see

ASBC Beer-29 and 44). Different setups will be used for the different classes of material, most notably the detector that is used to register the various species as they emerge from the column. For instance, a flame photometric detector has long been used to detect sulfur-containing substances, and lately chemiluminescence detection has also been used.

Measurement of Flavorsome Nonvolatiles

Materials that are nonvolatile are not measured by GC. Rather, they are typically measured by liquid chromatographic techniques, notably HPLC. These materials will include sugars, bitter acids, organic acids, and polyphenols. Polyphenols can also be measured colorimetrically (ASBC Beer-35).

A Feast of Variables

Chapter 7

In case you were in any doubt, even the most superficial reading of chapter 5 should have convinced you that "it ain't simple." If we were winemakers, we would accept change, stipulate the bare minimum (namely, grape varietal), and let nature take its course with our products, perhaps blending batches of wine to pay lip service to standardization and then declaring whether we had a good vintage or not. But we are brewers, and we seek consistency, at least within our notion of tolerable limits (see chapter 1).

We realize straightaway that many of the flavor notes will impact upon one another. In this I mean not so much how one might mask another (see, for example, the story about DMS in chapter 5, footnote 3), but rather insofar as how if we tweak a process to regulate the delivery of one note, that modification will likely change the aroma or taste derived from another entity. To illustrate, say we sought to lessen the DMS levels in our beer by choosing to lower somewhat the modification of our malt. That might manifest itself in a lessening of the amino acid level in the wort and lead to an increased production of higher alcohols that might then spill over into an elevated level of the still more flavor-active esters.

We must be ever mindful of this complication and the myriad of others: to change a process in the interests of regulating one flavor-active component may well have a more broad-brush impact on aroma and taste than we would want.

For these reasons, then, we must ultimately be mindful of our target flavor spectrum when we develop a new product and carefully define the raw material specifications (including barley and hop varieties and yeast strains) and process specifications (times, temperatures, aeration, equipment, and so on) that led us to that flavor profile. These specifications will be our foundation, on the basis of which we should only be making tweaks here and there if any aroma or taste notes drift.

It is not unheard of for brewers to think (usually for economic reasons) that they can, in short order, swap processes or ingredients without it having an impact on the flavor of the beer. Two examples follow.

A brewer was conducting trials with the goal of replacing a lauter tun with a mash filter. The brewer approached it with the naïve assumption that "wort is wort is wort," so the major impact would be a shorter turnaround time. Not so. First, the wort was brighter than that from the lauter tun, and this impacted yeast performance. Second, the finer grind in the hammer mill led to a greater extraction of the starch-degrading enzymes that were able to produce a more fermentable wort.

The second example concerns a brewer who closely monitored the price of sugar. Their choice of which adjunct to use—cane sugar (sucrose) or corn sugar (high-maltose syrup)—was entirely driven by cost, and they swapped between the two depending on which was cheaper at any given time. But yeast performs differently when presented with sucrose as opposed to maltose, with a concomitant influence on flavor. Seemingly, they could live with this aroma difference, which again speaks to philosophy in the way that we explored in chapter 1.

Mindful of these concepts, let us delve into the impact that process conditions can have on the key flavor determinants that we considered in chapter 5. I present my thoughts in two tables. Table 7-1 lists the approaches that will increase the expression of each particular note or level of each substance; the reader can intuit to take the converse approach to lower a given character. Table 7-2 focuses on reducing levels of some generally objectionable characters, such as VDKs. The tables also indicate the additional impacts that might be expected, so that the brewer enters mindfully into making any changes. Within the tables, the most logical approach (the one to try first) is highlighted in bold print. If there is no bold print under a given characteristic, that is a strong indication not to delve into this area lightly.

TABLE 7-1.

Approaches to Increasing Levels of Components or Perceived Flavor Notes

Approaches	Considerations
Bitterness	
Increased addition of hops, hop pellets, or hop extracts to the kettle.	This rise will be accompanied by an increased delivery of polyphenols into the wort (except for the extracts), increasing the risk of colloidal instability in the beer (see the upcoming volume on haze). This instability is especially the case if using lower α-acid hops. Some would argue increased hops addition will increase the mouthfeel of the beer.
Increase the length of the boil, remembering the guideline that, at 100°C and pH 5.2, approximately 1% of the α-acid is isomerized per minute.	This lengthening will lead to an increased breakdown of the dimethyl sulfide (DMS) precursor *S*-methylmethionine, thereby modifying DMS character (see DMS in Table 7-2). There will also be a risk of increased development of cooked character and some color development, as well as an inevitable concentration of the wort.
Addition of preisomerized bittering agents postfermentation.	Some argue that these materials detract from drinkability, although the reasons are less than clear. Some argue that the quality of bitterness is different and that some preparations give a harsh bitterness. If there is no hop bitter material in the wort, that increases the risk of microbiological spoilage in the brewery. Extracts need to be checked for gushing potential (see the first volume in this series, *Foam*).
Sourness[a]	
Lower the buffering potential of the wort (which is mostly owing to degradation products of protein), such that the acid produced by yeast does not get neutralized.	This lowering would most readily be achieved by replacing malt with non–protein containing adjunct, but that would fundamentally impact diverse flavors, both malt- and yeast-derived. Also, removing any low-temperature stage in mashing would lessen the production of buffering components.

[a] Unexpected and excessive sourness is an indicator of contamination with acid-forming bacteria.
[b] For most beers the aim is to avoid clove aroma. The overriding requirement in that case is to avoid wild yeasts.

continued

TABLE 7-1. continued

Approaches to Increasing Levels of Components or Perceived Flavor Notes

Approaches	Considerations
Acidify wort, by adding acids such as phosphoric or lactic (in the latter instance, it is traditional German practice to employ lactic acid bacteria for this purpose). Reduce the residual alkalinity of brewing water by reducing bicarbonate levels (acidification of the water) or increasing calcium levels.	Acidified mashes may be more fermentable through the increased release in an active form of limit dextrinase. Hop utilization is less at lower pHs, and there may be changes in the quality of the break. Wort pH can also influence the ability of yeast to produce some volatiles; for example, more DMS is produced at higher pHs. Wort pH also influences the rate at which vicinal diketone (VDK) precursors break down: breakdown is encouraged by lower pHs.
Enhance the vigor of yeast growth. (Note: it has been argued that changes to wort pH are much less significant regarding final beer pH than is the extent to which yeast produces acid during fermentation.)	Consideration of all the parameters that stimulate yeast growth (increased oxygen, increased temperature, addition of zinc, increased rousing, and increased pitching rate), but of course each of these would be expected to have an impact on the extent to which yeast delivers other flavor volatiles.
Acidification of the beer postfermentation.	Hygiene status.
Sweetness	
Use of nonfermentable sugars in the grist, notably lactose.	Possible change in other flavor notes, especially for more gently flavored beers.
Addition of priming sugars.	Increased susceptibility to microbial growth.
Addition of artificial sweeteners.	Legislation.
Use of "enzymic sweetening," namely, the addition of enzymes that will degrade the dextrins that survive fermentation.	Difficult to control. Also, if active enzyme survives the exercise, it precludes blending of the beer with any other beer that is not destined for enzymic priming.

continued

TABLE 7-1. continued

Approaches to Increasing Levels of Components or Perceived Flavor Notes

Approaches	Considerations
Not fermenting to completion.	Potential impact on other flavors, notably VDK control.
Using a yeast strain with less fermentative capability.	A different yeast is likely to deliver a different balance of other flavor entities.
Salts	
Adding defined quantities of commercial salt preparations.	Remember that positively charged ions are balanced with negatively charged ones. So, for example, addition of calcium as calcium sulfate will increase sulfate levels as well as calcium. If you use calcium chloride, you will increase chloride levels. If sulfate and chloride levels concern you, be mindful! Also be mindful of the purity of the preparations and ensure that there is no risk of elevating levels of ions such as iron, copper, and manganese.
Esters	
Select a yeast strain that is especially ester producing.	Implications for other aspects of flavor.
Lessening the amount of oxygen supplied to the yeast in fermentation.	Potential increase in level of short-chain fatty acids.
Using wort of increased clarity (i.e., remove more of the break material prior to fermentation).	Potential increase in level of short-chain fatty acids.
Decrease pitching rate.	Other impacts on fermentation parameters.
Increase the gravity of the wort to be pitched with control of alcohol by adding deaerated water downstream (namely, high-gravity brewing).	Risk of decreased foam stability through increased yeast stress.

continued

TABLE 7-1. continued

Approaches to Increasing Levels of Components or Perceived Flavor Notes

Approaches	Considerations
Increase the proportion of sugars in relation to amino acids in the wort, for example, by replacing more of the malt with adjuncts such as high-maltose syrup, glucose, or sucrose.	Impacts on other flavor volatiles; for example, DMS levels may also be increased.
Use open, shallow fermenters as opposed to deeper closed vessels.	Greater hygiene concerns.
Higher alcohols	
Consider a different yeast strain, especially an ale variant. Yeasts differ enormously in their ability to make higher alcohols.	Impact on other parameters by changing yeast.
Increase the oxygen availability to the yeast.	Will decrease esters.
Increase the level of zinc added to the fermenter.	Stimulating fermentation will impact other flavor molecules.
Increase fermentation temperature.	Will impact other aroma features.
Agitate the fermenter contents.	Risk to yeast integrity.
Reduce levels of free amino nitrogen in the wort.	Will impact other aroma features.
Increase levels of free amino nitrogen in the wort.	Will impact other aroma features.
Use more turbid wort.	Will impact other aroma features.
Use open, shallow fermenters as opposed to deeper closed vessels (lower hydrostatic pressure).	Greater hygiene concerns.

continued

TABLE 7-1. continued

Approaches to Increasing Levels of Components or Perceived Flavor Notes

Approaches	Considerations
4-Vinylguiaicol (clove)[b]	
Boost ferulic acid levels in wort by mashing in at a lower temperature (e.g., 45°C).	Increased complexity of operations; some argue for risk from proteolysis to parameters such as foam.
Select a hefeweissen strain that is a strong producer.	A different yeast will bring with it other flavor differences, although if you are specifically seeking to produce an authentic hefeweissen, it is likely that you are primarily concentrating on clove and banana (see esters).

TABLE 7-2.

Approaches to Decreasing Levels of Components or Perceived Flavor Notes

Approaches	Considerations
Vicinal diketones (VDKs)	
Ensure that there is a sufficient quantity of healthy yeast at the start, during fermentation, and at the end of fermentation to mop up VDKs. For example, don't use yeast that has been through many generations. Carefully select yeast from cones of fermenters. Younger, more virile cells will tend to be at the top of the cone.	The yeast will need to be removed as soon as VDKs (and acetaldehyde) have been dealt with to avoid foam problems.
Allow a temperature rise of 1–2°C midway through primary fermentation.	Elevating temperature may also boost the production of higher alcohols, which may spill over into increased ester levels.
Increase the oxygen supply to the yeast.	Ester levels will decrease.
Decrease the level of adjuncts that do not contain nitrogen (e.g., sugars and syrups).	Will impact other flavors.
Ensure wort pH is less than 5.2, which will decrease precursor production.	If lower wort pH translates into lower beer pH, that will decrease flavor stability of the beer.
Increase the yeast count at the end of primary fermentation (kräusening).	If the yeast is not as healthy as it should be, that risks autolysis and secretion of damaging enzymes.
Selection of a yeast strain that produces less VDK or that has an increased predilection to scavenge VDKs, for example, by being less flocculent.	A different yeast will probably give a different balance of other flavors.
Allow prolonged contact with "green" beer and yeast to mop up final traces of VDKs.	This will do nothing for the foam and may lead to a decrease in foam performance (see the first volume in the series, *Foam*).
Employ the Sinebrychoff process, wherein green beer is heated to 80°C for 4 min to break down the precursors, followed by passage of the beer through a column of immobilized active yeast cells.	It is critical that the oxygen level and yeast count be as low as possible, otherwise there will be negative flavor impact.
Include the enzyme acetolactate decarboxylase in fermentation.	On-cost.

continued

TABLE 7-2. continued

Approaches to Decreasing Levels of Components or Perceived Flavor Notes

Approaches	Considerations
Ensure an absence of diacetyl-producing microorganisms at all stages in the brewery and bar.	
Short-chain fatty acids (SFAs)	
Change to an ale strain, as they tend to produce lower levels of SFAs.	Impact on other parameters by changing yeast.
Increase the oxygen availability to the yeast.	Will decrease esters.
Present the yeast with turbid worts.	Will impact other aroma features.
Increase the amount of non–nitrogen containing adjunct to increase the ratio of carbon to nitrogen.	Will impact other flavor volatiles.
Avoid recovering beer from yeast slurries.	Increased losses and effluent.
Dimethyl sulfide (DMS)	
Decrease the S-methylmethionine (SMM) level in the grist (replacement of malt with adjuncts, decreased modification of malt, use of rootlet inhibitor, increased intensity of kilning, selecting a two-row as opposed to a six-row variety).	Obvious impacts of changing the grist. Less modification and more kilning means, for example, increased β-glucan risks.
Increased duration and vigor of the kettle boil.	Some concern about increased cooked character. Fifty percent of the precursor is converted to DMS in 38 min at pH 5.2 and 32.5 min at pH 5.5. So wort pH impacts, as does altitude: the higher the altitude, the less rapidly the SMM will be broken down.
Reduced residence time in the hot wort receiver.	Impact on wort clarity. If trub is not efficiently removed, then the increased turbidity can impact yeast metabolism and production of other flavor volatiles.
Use of wort stripper.	Will also purge other volatiles.
Use of open, shallow fermenters.	Greater hygiene concerns.
Increase in fermentation temperature.	Will impact other aroma substances.

continued

TABLE 7-2. continued

Approaches to Decreasing Levels of Components or Perceived Flavor Notes

Approaches	Considerations
Ensure an absence of DMS-producing wort spoilage microorganisms in the brewhouse.	Will also lessen risk from nonvolatile nitrosamines.
Hydrogen sulfide	
Ensure vigorous fermentation, for example, healthy yeast, sufficient oxygen, sufficient zinc, and turbulence (which will be promoted in more turbid wort). Doing so will also promote the removal of other sulfides.	Impact on some other aroma substances.
Lower levels of sulfate and sulfite in the wort.	
Caution with selection of material for dry hopping.	
Add copper ions.	Copper is a prooxidant and also (if inadvertently added to excess) a poison.
Avoid any conditions that will promote yeast autolysis.	
Skunk (from 3-methyl-2-butene-1-thiol)	
Packaging in brown glass bottles or cans.	Bisphenol A concerns with cans.
Use of reduced side-chain iso-α-acids.	Differences in perceived quantity and quality of bitterness. Changes in foam texture (see the first volume, *Foam*).
Avoid risk of introducing any (and I mean *any*) conventional hop iso-α-acids into wort or beer destined for producing a light-resistant beer for packaging in anything other than brown glass. For example, attend to the rigor of clean-in-place regimes, look for any opportunity for carryover of material such as trub, schedule the "light resistant" beers first through a filter, and so on.	Worts and beers bittered with reduced iso-α-acids cannot contact any conventionally hopped worts and beers, because even tiny quantities of conventional hops will be sufficient to give a distinct skunky character.
Use of riboflavin-binding proteins.	Not readily available.
Logistics that preclude exposure of beer in clear, green, or blue glass to natural or artificial light.	Bottled beer is invariably stocked in bars in glass-fronted, well-lit refrigerated cabinets.

continued

TABLE 7-2. continued

Approaches to Decreasing Levels of Components or Perceived Flavor Notes

Approaches	Considerations
Acetaldehyde	
Use open, shallow fermenters.	Greater hygiene concerns.
Ensure vigorous fermentation, for example, healthy yeast, sufficient oxygen, sufficient zinc, and turbulence (which will be promoted in more turbid wort).	Impact on other aroma substances.
Avoid premature yeast–beer separation.	Prolonged yeast–beer contact is not good for foam.
Boost SO_2 levels.	Avoid going over 10 mg/L, at which level the beer must be labeled "contains sulfites" in the United States.
Ensure an absence of acetaldehyde-producing microorganisms, notably *Zymomonas* spp., which are particularly a problem with primed beers.	
Grainy/astringent	
Minimize agitation in mashing, which leads to scraping of astringent materials off husk.	There will be less extraction of substances such as silicon. Risk of less efficient extraction of beneficial materials.
Avoid prolonging wort separation to collect ever lower gravities—such weak worts will be rich in grainy materials.	Extract yield will be less—and if weak worts are sent to the drain, increased biological oxygen demand in the environment.
Ensure that pH does not rise excessively as the buffering potential of worts at lower gravities decreases. Avoid high carbonate levels. Use calcium.	
Musty	
Taste or smell all materials, notably malt, to ensure no musty off-character is entering into the brew. Don't forget packaging materials, pallets, and so on.	Don't try to taste materials that are unsafe, such as cleaning agents.
Use carbon filtration for all water.	Must have a maintenance program for the filter.

continued

TABLE 7-2. continued

Approaches to Decreasing Levels of Components or Perceived Flavor Notes

Approaches	Considerations
Avoid musty areas in the brewery, because those aromas can be picked up by raw materials, packaging materials, and so on, as well as the risk of key tasters becoming used to it and therefore somewhat blind to it in the beer.	
Stringent attention to hygiene, cleaning systems, avoidance of dead legs (pipes and other structures that are not reached by cleaning solutions), and so on.	
Antiseptic/plastic	
Do not use water with a distinct chlorinated character—if present, remove by carbon filtration or perhaps boiling.	
Avoid use of chlorine-containing cleaning agents/sterilants.	This recommendation does not absolve the brewer from using cleaning agents or sterilants. Choose those that work for you.
Cheesy	
Careful selection and cold storage of hop products.	

Aroma Kits Appendix **1**

Aroxa

Bill Simpson really started the aroma standards concept in brewing, and the Campden BRI and FlavorActiV products were spawned from his genius. His latest company is Aroxa. An example of one of the Aroxa kits is illustrated in Figure A-1. Each flavor is accompanied by a

Fig. A-1. A flavor and aroma training kit. Photo courtesy of Aroxa.

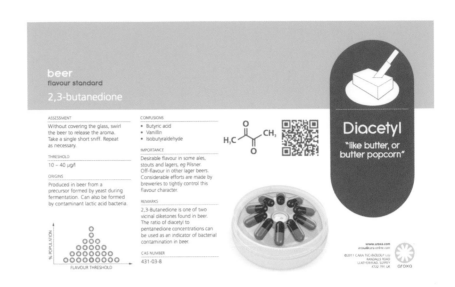

Fig. A-2. A card describing diacetyl. Image courtesy of Aroxa.

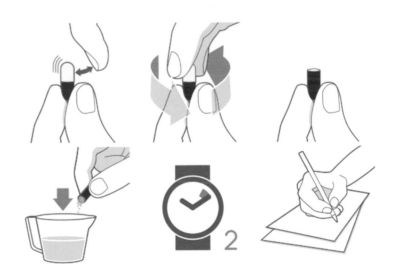

Fig. A-3. Visual instructions for using the flavor and aroma capsules. Image courtesy of Aroxa.

descriptive card (Fig. A-2). The standards are easy to use (Fig. A-3) and associated with a simple tasting form (Fig. A-4).

www.aroxa.com

The tasting form table with attributes:

| control | acetaldehyde (acetaldehyde) | acetic (acetic acid) | almond (benzaldehyde) | butyric (butyric acid) | catty (p-menthane-8-thiol-3-one) | chlorophenol (2,6-dichlorophenol) | diacetyl (2,3-butanedione) | DMS (dimethyl sulphide) | ethyl butyrate (ethyl butyrate) | ethyl hexanoate (ethyl hexanoate) | freshly cut grass (cis-3-hexanol) | geraniol (geraniol) | grainy (isobutyraldehyde) |

| H2S (hydrogen sulphide) | isoamyl acetate (isoamyl acetate) | isovaleric (isovaleric acid) | kettle hop (kettle hop extract) | lightstruck (3-methyl-2-butene-1-thiol) | mercaptan (ethanethiol) | metallic (ferrous sulphate) | musty (2,4,6-trichloroanisole) | onion (dimethyl trisulphide) | papery (trans-2-nonenal) | phenolic (4-vinyl guaiacol) | sour (citric acid) | sulphitic (sulphur dioxide) | vanilla (vanillin) |

Fig. A-4. The tasting form that accompanies the kit. The form is used for scoring the intensity of flavor for each attribute. A low level of a character would result in a box being checked close to the left, perhaps the yellow line if there is little or none. Intense levels would result in a box checked further to the right. Image courtesy of Aroxa.

Campden BRI

www.bri-advantage.com/services/sensory/sensory6a.php

FlavorActiV

www.flavoractiv.com

Siebel Institute of Technology

www.siebelinstitute.com

The cost of Siebel Institute's sensory training kit is subsidized for Beer Judge Certification Program exam preparation.

www.bjcp.org/cep/kits.php

Some Taste Training Opportunities

Alex Barlow, www.allbeer.co.uk
Beer Academy, www.beeracademy.co.uk/courses
Susan Langstaff, www.appliedsensory.com
Roy Desrochers, www.geiconsultants.com
Siebel Institute of Technology, www.siebelinstitute.com
Bill Simpson, www.cara-online.com

Further Reading

Chapter 1

Bamforth, C. W. (2011) Beer Is Proof God Loves Us: Reaching for the Soul of Beer and Brewing. Financial Times Press, Upper Saddle River, NJ.

Bamforth, C. W., Butcher, K. N., and Cope, R. (1989) The interrelationships between parameters of beer quality. Ferment 2:54–58.

Reading *Beer Is Proof God Loves Us* will put the author's philosophy into context, including the significance of beer flavor. If you do read it, be sure to read the main part first and the endnotes separately, especially if reading on Kindle.

Chapter 2

Chartier, F. (2012) Taste Buds and Molecules: The Art and Science of Food, Wine, and Flavor. Wiley, Hoboken, NJ.

Lawless, H. T., and Heymann, H. (1998) Sensory Evaluation of Food: Principles and Practices. Kluwer Academic/Plenum Publishers, New York, NY.

Rouby, C., Schaal, B., Dubois, D., Gervais, R., and Holley, A., eds. (2002) Olfaction, Taste, and Cognition. Cambridge University Press, Cambridge, U.K.

Chapter 3

American Society of Brewing Chemists. Beer Flavor Wheel. Available at: www.asbcnet.org/flavorwheel

Meilgaard, M. C., Dalgliesh, C. E., and Clapperton, J. F. (1979) Beer flavor terminology. J. Am. Soc. Brew. Chem. 37:47–52.

Meilgaard, M. C., Reid, D. S., and Wyborski, K. A. (1982) Reference standards for beer flavor terminology system. J. Am. Soc. Brew. Chem. 40:119–128.

Chapter 4

American Society of Brewing Chemists. ASBC Methods of Analysis, online. Am. Soc. Brew. Chem., St. Paul, MN.

Meilgaard, M. C., Carr, B. T., and Civille, G. V. (2006) Sensory Evaluation Techniques, 4th Ed. CRC Press, Boca Raton, FL.

Simpson, W. J. (2006) Brewing control systems: Sensory evaluation. In: Brewing: New Technologies. C. W. Bamforth, ed. Woodhead, Cambridge, U.K. pp. 427–460.

Chapter 5

Bamforth, C. W. (2006) Scientific Principles of Malting and Brewing. Am. Soc. Brew. Chem., St. Paul, MN.

Bamforth, C. W., ed. (2009) Beer: A Quality Perspective. Academic Press, Burlington, MA.

Briggs, D. E., Boulton, C. A., Brookes, P. A., and Stevens, R. (2004) Brewing: Science and Practice. Woodhead, Cambridge, U.K.

Donaldson, B. A., Bamforth, C. W., and Heymann, H. (2012) Sensory descriptive analysis and free-choice profiling of thirteen hop varieties as whole cones and after dry hopping of beer. J. Am. Soc. Brew. Chem. 70:176–181.

Jowitt, R. (1974) The terminology of food texture. J. Texture Stud. 5:351–358.

Kunze, W. (2010) Technology Brewing and Malting. VLB, Berlin, Germany.

Langstaff, S. A., and Lewis, M. J. (1993) The mouthfeel of beer—A review. J. Inst. Brew. 99:31–37.

Murray, J. P., Bennett, S. J. E., Chandra, G. S., Davies, N. J., and Pickles, J. L. (1999) Sensory analysis of malt. Tech. Q. Master Brew. Assoc. Am. 36:15–19.

Priest, F. G., and Stewart, G. G., eds. (2006) Handbook of Brewing. CRC Press, Boca Raton, FL.

Chapter 6

American Society of Brewing Chemists. ASBC Methods of Analysis, online. Am. Soc. Brew. Chem., St. Paul, MN.

Bamforth, C. W., Butcher, K. N., and Cope, R. (1989) The interrelationships between parameters of beer quality. Ferment 2:54–58.

U.S. Environmental Protection Agency. National Primary Drinking Water Regulations. Available at: http://water.epa.gov/drink/contaminants/index.cfm#Primary

Chapter 7

Casey, G. Fishbone References for Applied Brewing Scientists. Available at: www.asbcnet.org/fishbone

Casey, G. P. (2007) A journey in brewing science and the ASBC. In: Brewing Chemistry and Technology in the Americas. P. W. Gales, ed. Am. Soc. Brew. Chem., St. Paul, MN. pp. 192–202.

Greg Casey's fishbone diagrams for troubleshooting are available through these two sources.

Index